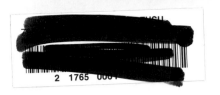

HOLISTIC RUNNING

HOLISTIC RUNNING

Beyond the Threshold of Fitness

by Joel Henning

With an Introduction from the
National Jogging Association

Atheneum   New York   1978

Library of Congress Cataloging in Publication Data
Henning, Joel.
    Holistic running.

    Bibliography: p.
    Includes index.
    1. Jogging. 2. Running. I. Title.
GV494.H47   1978   796.4 '26   78-3191
ISBN 0-689-10924-5

Copyright © 1978 by Joel Henning

Introduction copyright © 1978 by
The New American Library Inc.

Published simultaneously in Canada by
McClelland and Stewart Ltd.

Designed by Lorraine Hohman

First Edition

For AMH

Acknowledgments

Many people have helped in putting this book together. The editors of *Chicago Magazine* encouraged my first efforts to express deep feelings about running and helped polish the text of "Running Sacred," which appears here in altered form as Chapter One. Gary Olsen, executive director of the National Jogging Association, proposed that I consider doing a book. I thank him. Jeff Ballowe helped me find useful materials on subjects ranging from alveolar air to cardiovascular conditioning, and offered many good suggestions as the book took shape. Bruce Dern's comments on the manuscript and insights into running were very helpful. Dr. George R. Gabriel not only applied his podiatric skills to the maintenance and repair of my feet but also provided invaluable advice and commentary on the manuscript.

Dr. Noel D. Nequin, medical director of the Cardiac Rehabilitation Center of Swedish Covenant Hospital of Chicago, demonstrates the special qualities of holistic runners in his professional life and by his leadership in bringing joyful running events to his community. Noel gently pointed out muddles and errors in the text and helped me correct them. Another running doctor, Lowell Scott Weil, director of the Podiatric Sports Medicine Center of the Illinois College of Podiatric Medicine, was extraordinarily helpful as deadline time approached and questions lingered in my mind. Several improvements in the manuscript also resulted from comments by Lieutenant General (ret.) R. L. Bohannen, M.D., president of the National Jogging Association, and Dr. Elliot Kieff of the University of Chicago's Pritzker School of Medicine. Mary Alice Conlon and her staff at the Athlete's Foot store in Chicago's Loop helped me sort through mountains of running shoes to evaluate the most satisfactory models. Dr. George Sheehan has inspired me to run farther and write better. I wish I could do either as well as he.

Writing is often unpleasant and always lonely, but the preparation of clean, readable drafts, again and again through endless revisions, is even more unpleasant and lonely. I am grateful to Earnestine Murphy and Nancy Dwiel, who were able to tolerate my chaotic schedule and transform my left-handed scrawl into a coherent typescript.

I have come to depend on the sharp critiques and sensible editing my work receives from my wife, Grace. She is a tough critic, but a good one. For all she does and endures, I am especially indebted to her.

Contents

Introduction

What urge drives an otherwise normal person out of a warm bed in the dead of winter and into the pre-dawn cold? Or out of an air-conditioned office to run on a sweltering August afternoon? Surely there's more to running than keeping in shape. The benefits go beyond fitness. For many it's a total experience that can aptly be called holistic running.

For Joel Henning and perhaps millions of others, running is as much a mental and spiritual experience as it is an exquisitely physical pastime. The integration of the whole person—body, mind, and soul—in the activity of running can be a mystical experience. Besides the undeniable physical rewards it offers, running is a means to personal growth and an entree into higher states of consciousness.

It is a measure of how far the running movement has come that a book on holistic running is being published. When Dr. Richard Bohannon conceived the idea of the National Jogging Association and Gary K. Olsen opened the NJA doors in 1969, there were barely a handful of books on running and health. Today there are many. Yet *Holistic Running* stands out among them.

Joel Henning has written a unique book that explores the inner and outer spaces of running. Everything from footwear to fitness programs to meditation is covered.

Drawing on poetry, philosophy, and his own quest for self-discovery, Henning makes a lyrical personal statement that is bound to affect and motivate every reader of this highly recommended book. In the end, we cannot help but feel our "spirits rise with the sun," joining his. After all, as runners we "own the day."

—Bernard L. Gladieux, Jr.
editor, *The Jogger*
the magazine of the
National Jogging Association

1

Running Sacred:
Come Along and Feel It

My body of a sudden blazed;
And twenty minutes more or less
It seemed, so great my happiness,
That I was blessed, and could bless.

From "Vacillation"
by WILLIAM BUTLER YEATS

I am a runner. Four or five mornings a week I awake at 6:00 A.M., anoint my feet with Vaseline or tincture of benzoin or powder (or all three), cover my worst blisters with tape, and approach the jumble of sweat clothes, athletic socks, shorts, and mottled jockstrap that is draped over the portable TV in my bedroom, as if it were a primitive altar. In fact, it is the symbol of a kind of worship involving holy breathing, obtestation, propitiation, atonement, sacrifice, exorcism, karma, asanas, and meditation.

I transfer the raunchy costume from the TV set to my body, and then, in what is perhaps the most arcane moment in this ritual, I slip my vacuum-cast, leather-covered plastic orthotic appliances into my running shoes. Simultaneously, I mutter a prayer for the continued good health of my imaginative podiatrist. He custom-built these devices to correct the congenital forefoot varus that had afflicted me with plantar fasciitis, causing the most intense pain imaginable in my heels whenever I tried to run. I do not offer a prayer for the good doctor's prosperity, because that is assured so long as the devout are willing to kick in a hundred dollars and more for these things (which work like a charm, incidentally) and sweeten the kitty with frequent fifteen-dollar office visits for hydrotherapy, ultrasonic treatment, shoe counseling, and other forms of podiatric voodoo.

Next come the requisite rites. I drink a bathroom cup of water because I plan to run at least eight miles, and outdoor water fountains are no help in the winter. Most long-distance runners drink something before attempting to do more than five miles or so: I drink water because it is the liquid most efficiently put to use by the body. Other runners take anything from de-fizzed Coke to beer. In long races, liquid-refreshment stands are set up for the runners every three to five miles. They may offer water, cola, tea with honey, or one of several products concocted to provide quick energy by replacing something called electrolytes, which the body consumes during strenuous exercise. Dehydration and sunstroke probably give long-distance runners more trouble than anything except dogs and cars.

Then comes catharsis. If I am lucky, it will involve both my bladder and colon. If I have done my exercises—stretching and muscle building and yoga—I will have a better chance at success. But, for me at least, most exercising is best done on days when I don't run, or at least eight or ten hours before or after running. Muscle-building calisthenics especially, such as curls, push-ups, and leg-ups, make me feel heavy; my legs and feet, wobbly at the best of times, become so wobbly that I can't run at all. Still, nothing beats the combination of water and exercise for clearing the colon. Runners probably talk and fret more about their toilet habits than any group. Neither wind, nor sleet, nor hail will stem a runner, but an urgent biological need four miles down a cross-country course with not even a bush in sight, will, sure as hell.

Finally I hit the street, usually just before dawn. I run slowly down my street near the University of Chicago, toward Lake Michigan. My muscles are still cold. My disposition is sour and not improved by residual aromas of the past evening that emanate from the local Mexican restaurant and pizza parlor.

The pace quickens through Jackson Park, where I am spurred on by the voluptuous caryatids on the Museum of Science and Industry—my groupies. Their spirits seem to protect me from the nettlesome little dogs being walked by biddies in hair curlers.

Next, I accept the challenge of crossing Hyde Park Boulevard, where the mostly empty city buses driven by sadists are a major hazard. I slow down, they slow down; I attempt a crossing, they rush at me. But I prevail and regain a steady pace. The sweat begins to rise.

"Second wind" is approaching. Yes, there *is* a second wind; I will swear to its existence. Physiological data verify it. Japanese scientists put the Olympic gold medal marathon-runner Abebe Bikila on a treadmill. After three minutes of running, his heart and respiratory rates stopped rising and began to decline. As his pulse and breathing slowed, he began to sweat and his blood pressure decreased. With me, it takes longer than three minutes—usually somewhere between five and six—but when second wind comes, it brings with it the first stage of my running "high." I feel better, my speed increases, my breathing assumes a slower, steadier rhythm, and my muscles begin to get warm—signals of more pleasure to come.

Turning north, I follow the bridle path along Lake Shore Drive to a pedestrian underpass. I run down the embankment and east into the dark tunnel, using the eerie echoes to assess how efficiently my feet are dealing with the pavement. A soft thud is all I hope to hear as my heels make contact. Too often, though, there is a ridiculous slap as I come down flat-footed, failing to roll from heel to toe.

Most people, including salesmen for athletic shoes, wrongly think that a runner should run on his toes. This is only so with sprinters and some middle-distance runners. Running on the toes is faster, but it puts enormous strain on the leg muscles. Long-distance runners and joggers are prime candidates for shinsplints and worse if they don't use a stride that brings the foot down heel first, so as to cushion it from an average of 1,600 brutalizing strikes per mile.

Running through the underpass, it occurs to me that this sort of dark recess is where I am most likely to be mugged. Oh my God, a body! Relief a second later. Only a sleeping bum . . . My heart recovers from the sudden fright. I recall that in several years of running along Chicago's south lake shore, New York's Central Park, Washington's malls, the beaches of Venice, California, and other battlegrounds, no one has even given me a nasty look. But David Gottlieb, a marathon runner who lives in the Maryland suburbs of the District of Columbia, was ambushed by two hoodlums and hit in the face with a rock while running. He suffered an aneurysm near his brain. Victor Krol was shot in the thigh while training for a marathon in Chicago. Neither incident involved robbery.

Just wanton sadism. I hear such reports and wonder at the idiocy (or perversity) of the attackers. When I run, I carry nothing of value; in fact I carry nothing at all except a sweaty T-shirt in summer, for mopping my face. These are slim pickings, to say the least.

Women runners have more problems; some have even reported attacks by other runners. Dr. Joan Ullyot, a champion marathoner, advises women to avoid running alone and to carry little cans of Macelike dog repellent known as Halt. I am often tempted to get some for myself, especially when I run in rural areas, where the risk is greatest of being menaced or chewed by dogs.

Coming out of the tunnel, I turn north and really begin to run. I am within five yards of Lake Michigan. Only a storm or ice can drive me up against the fence bounding the highway. One morning, a wave came up over the puny embankment and nearly carried me back with it into the lake. But now the sun is beginning to free itself from the horizon, diffidently at first, gaining confidence and intensity as it achieves independence from the lake. And my spirits rise with the sun.

The sunrise inspired runners Dr. Arthur Jay Mollen and Peggy Lynn Armstrong to wed at 5:30 A.M. on the summit of Arizona's Squaw Peak. The wedding party of seventy-five, including running Rabbi Frederick Grosse, all ran up the mountain for the ceremony. Tom McGrath and his bride ran 3,046 miles across the United States on their honeymoon. They broke the transcontinental running record, finishing in fifty-three days. Why not? I remember a run through London's beautiful Hyde Park and Kensington Gardens, where I passed an African, a graduate student probably. He was running but he was also dancing, doing graceful turns and arabesques. He was also smiling, laughing, and shouting. In London! We runners are like children: free to run and dance, even free to shout. Who ruled that adults must walk?

I approach an embankment, the nearest thing to a hill in Chicago. My attention focuses on breathing—belly breathing. Force the diaphragm in to push out the carbon dioxide, relax and let the morning air rush into the lungs. Morning runs offer the best air, before it is loaded with the full day's pollution.

Carbon monoxide (CO) is a more serious threat to runners than muggers. It is normally present in outdoor air in a concentration of three to four parts per million (ppm). Automobile exhaust contains 5,000 to 7,000 ppm, while the level in a cigarette smoker's lungs is 40–50,000 ppm. In a recent study reported in the *Annals of Internal Medicine*, running performance at different concentrations of carbon monoxide were compared. For each increase in CO concentration, there was almost a threefold decrease in runners' performance. The CO level during an early-morning run along Chicago's Lake Shore Drive or on the roadways through New York's Central Park, however, is probably only about 25 ppm.

Dr. George Sheehan, a first-class runner, heart specialist, medical advisor to thousands, and an elegant writer, advises us folks in places like Chicago, Cleveland, and New York to run brazenly right through the CO blitz. CO binds to hemoglobin and lowers the body's available oxygen capacity. Running in CO pollution, then, is like running at higher altitudes in Denver or Mexico City. But the only way to get rid of the stuff is to exhale it; a runner does so at a considerably more efficient rate than a smoker or an automobile driver.

Ozone alerts present another, less considered, threat. Caused by petrochemical smog, they seem to occur in our big cities with increasing frequency each summer. I can generally tell when there will be an ozone alert before hearing the news report because my run has left me more tired and less exhilarated than usual.

This morning, though, the air seems relatively pure, and I push on toward the top of the rise, thinking about my stride. Run from the hips and thighs, strike with the heel, roll to the toe, and push off. Run as erectly as possible; don't lean forward or crouch. Pretend that your head is attached to a skyhook. Focus your eyes on a distant object to help keep your head steady and your shoulders relaxed. Keep your arms at your hips, hands in loose fists. All the action in your arms should come from the elbows, while your shoulders are relaxed and remain relatively inactive. Relax, relax. Start relaxing by keeping your jaw loose. Pretend that a rope is connected to your center of gravity, a few inches below the navel, and that it is being reeled in from a point way out in front.

It sounds like a lot to remember, but it is very little compared with all that I fail to hold in my head while skiing or playing tennis. Running is, after all, the most natural of human activities. It requires less equipment and paraphernalia than any other sport except swimming, which is also natural. It is no coincidence that these two activities consistently rate highest in their contributions to fitness. To improve my form, I imagine a TV image of Frank Shorter and Waldemar Cierpinski running the '76 Olympic marathon through the streets of Montreal, gliding along with easy elegance and style. For a minute, I am Frank Shorter, one of America's best marathon runners, until all thought is

scattered; I concentrate on working my lungs and legs
to the top of the rise.

Up here I get my first panoramic look at the city.
White and red ribbons of head- and tail-lights cover
the eight lanes of Lake Shore Drive. The lake is the
palest of blues, except for the gentle ripples and
waves, which rise to take a touch of pink from the
dawn sun. Strobe lights flash on a dark runway out on
the peninsula airport, Meigs Field. Looming up behind
it all is the architectural forest of downtown Chicago,
where scattered lights are blinking up and down the
modern towers. The sky is a very faint rosy blue,
making the scene look like something out of grand
opera—artificially lit and unrealistic, but appealing nevertheless. As fellow runner Richard Strebech says,
"Everything is prettier when you're running." Strebech is seventy-four. He runs four to five miles every
day. He started when he was sixty-three.

As I run down the embankment, I catch up with
my own favorite superannuated runner, Townes.
Townes is sixty years old and lives in one of the ghet-
tos that begin within a quarter mile of the beautiful
lakefront. Every day he runs twenty miles. Last year
he entered his first marathon (26 miles, 385 yards)
and finished it ahead of lots of runners carrying many
fewer years. Townes makes me seem slothful; on
weekdays I usually go only eight or nine miles. On
the other hand, I don't spend more than a few minutes
being convivial with Townes because my comfortable
pace is a bit faster than his.

The difference between Townes's pace and mine is
the difference between jogging and running. A jogger
is trotting along at a pace of nine minutes or more per
mile. A runner is doing the same thing, only faster. I
average between seven and eight minutes per mile.

Waldemar Cierpinski won the 1976 Olympic marathon in just under two hours and ten minutes, or less than five minutes per mile, for more than twenty-six miles! My pace is closer to jogging than it is to world-class long-distance running, but for anyone not in competition, the best pace is a convivial one—so you can talk with a fellow runner or jogger.

At the sociable pace of seven or eight minutes per mile, your body's ability to function efficiently increases on a pay-as-you-go or "aerobic" basis, a term made popular almost a decade ago by the publication of Dr. Kenneth Cooper's book, *Aerobics*. Basically, Cooper's theory is that highly stressful activity by an untrained body produces an *an*aerobic effect, meaning that the activity is accomplished without a sufficient supply of oxygen and therefore only with some damage to the body. Even a well-trained athlete suffers anaerobic effects in competition from pushing himself beyond his body's capacity to function effectively on the oxygen he can take in as he runs. But jogging or running at your own pace, for fun and exercise, is an aerobic activity, which means that you breathe in the amount of oxygen needed for the energy expended, and your body is better off for having done it. Dr. Cooper believes that, after a few weeks of conditioning, you can fulfill your need for aerobic exercise by running three miles in 43.5 minutes or less, five times a week. This modest program will yield thirty points on Cooper's aerobic scale—enough, he says, to provide some protection from heart disease.

Some enthusiasts, including Dr. Sheehan, think that Cooper discourages many people from taking up jogging and running by boring them with tables, charts, points, and scientific jargon. In *The Zen of Running*, Fred Rohe says the same thing Cooper does, but in the language of Zen. "By running with your breath," he writes, "you store a surplus of *prana*, a Sanskrit word meaning Absolute Energy, the invisible vital force which supplies the primal motivation for every form of activity." I call my way "holistic running," meaning that it is good for the body and also helps expand awareness of oneself and the rest of the world, much like certain Zen and yoga rituals.

For starters, you may find that your comfortable pace is a mile walk. And then gradually it may become a mile done in combination walk and jog. No coach or doctor or guru can prescribe the proper pace for you. Things have not changed since the great Galen, who served as physician to Marcus Aurelius, said that "the right degree must be found in practice. It cannot be expressed in writing."

Try going out every other day. I'm certain that having to maintain a daily schedule would have quickly turned me into a dropout. A three- or four-day-per-week exercise program can keep you fit, even if it cannot prepare you for the Boston marathon.

I started running seriously about five years ago, at age thirty-three. At first, two laps around the University of Chicago track was a splendid achievement. Before the year was out, I was up to two miles. Gradually, I *wanted* to run farther: four miles, then six. Now I feel best when I go at least eight, which is the maximum I can run on a weekday and still be in my office by 9:00 A.M. Six to eight miles is long enough to bring me to the level of holistic running at which I get beyond ordinary consciousness and enter into a kind of trance. On weekends I will run anywhere from six to twenty miles, depending on my mood, the weather, the season, and my social plans.

I reserve running on the track, incidentally, to occasions when I want to time myself for interval training (no more often than once a week), or when the rest of the world is mud, or when the wind and waves make the lakefront seem like the edge of Hell. Running indoors has about as much appeal to me as skiing indoors. It can be done, and I have done it in rainy cities like Seattle, but what a bore.

Heading toward the lake, I run alternately on the grass and on the asphalt walks, avoiding the most uneven patches of turf for fear of turning an ankle, which I do with monotonous regularity. Suddenly a Doberman pinscher springs from behind nearby shrubbery and challenges me. I have two routines for dogs. If I think they can be intimidated, I do my "top dog" act, in which I menace them with waving arms and lots of growling, asserting my position in the pack as top dog. If I am convincing, the dog cowers and slinks away. But if I suspect that the dog himself lays claim to the top spot in the pack, as in this case, I freeze. I always freeze for Dobermans. Finally, the owner arrives and secures the leash, apologizing at length. I wait until the leash is on and then start up again, muttering threats about guns, Mace, and police.

But all this is purged from my mind within seconds of resuming my pace. When running, you can't attend to frustrations or anger. Running demands easy and pleasant thoughts. There is no way to run efficiently, expand your consciousness, and think bad thoughts at the same time. And perhaps because no extra energy is available for the part of the mind reserved for bad thoughts, they are driven out or merely dissolve. This accounts for much of the popularity of running and some of its therapeutic effects, too. I can work through easy problems while running, but I can't dwell on irresolvable dilemmas. I might have insights, but I won't be able to sustain long, logical thought structures. One marathoner says he builds houses in his head as he runs. Another says he can think about making love, but not about complicated love affairs. According to Bill Rodgers, who won the '76 and '77 New York marathons, a runner mainly has to concentrate on keeping in touch with his or her body. Opera star Robert Merrill claims to be able to learn lyrics as he jogs. I might attempt to count the number of Volvos in proportion to the total number of cars on a nearby road, but my arithmetic falls like a house of cards when the number gets to be much over fifty. Then, in the advanced stages of holistic running, I am beyond numbers and words.

Here is my turnaround, McCormick Place, Chicago's major convention hall. In spite of my resistance to bad thoughts, this massive structure never fails to depress me. It looks like a coffin for the Colossus of Rhodes. Its size enervates anyone coming near. I seem to be running on a treadmill, getting no closer. But then I veer to the east, where Burnham Harbor separates McCormick Place from Meigs Field, and encounter a world of human dimensions and pastoral charm. Several people are fishing. Bicycle riders are resting on the lawns and benches. A man is photographing the little planes coming in and out of Meigs Field. Cops are kibitzing with the fishermen. If McCormick Place is like a rock, this little area reminds me of the bustling activity often found when such a rock is turned over.

My turnaround point is the north end of McCormick Place. I start back through the underground passage that reaches the entire length of the building. Here I receive the stares of taxi drivers, convention exhibitors, and watchmen. The contrast between the inert beginnings of their day and the dynamic overture to mine gives me some satisfaction.

The feeling is like the one that I get when, in Washington, D.C., I run from the Hay-Adams Hotel, through Lafayette Park, across Pennsylvania Avenue, and then around the North and East gates of the White House. I see nervous security men keeping me under observation and tracking my course by telephone. Is he a jogger or an Arab terrorist? Early-rising plutocrats, bellboys, and house detectives are also curious when I return to the Plaza Hotel in New York, sweating and exhausted, after a run in Central Park. One time I returned to find the Plaza's house detective about to use his passkey to enter my room. I had gotten up early and left before the operator rang the room as I had requested the night before. When she got no answer at 6:00 A.M., the hotel dick assumed I was a victim of something or other. He looked up at me *in extremis* after my run and was more convinced than ever that something was very wrong.

The only place where no one ever seems to be interested is the Strip in Las Vegas. At dawn, croupiers and waitresses wait for buses, and gamblers trudge from the casino where they lost to the next, where they will surely win. They must think I am engaged in a pre-game ritual, for luck. Maybe they're right.

As I come out of the McCormick Place tunnel back into daylight, the southwest wind hits me at fourteen miles per hour. The effect is like running uphill, only worse. My body is chilled and I wish that I had worn gloves. The wind strips away some of my pleasure, making it painfully clear that I have already run between four and fives miles. I am in that uncomfortable stage between a mere fitness run and a holistic experience, when the physical body would like to call it a day and the spiritual self has not yet become active. The sense of easy, gliding grace that brought me this far was partly the result of a tail wind.

I feel minor aches, the beginnings of tiredness in my back. My feet, bless them, are still content. They have been very well cushioned by a good pair of running shoes, the only serious investment that a runner or jogger must make.

Like most beginners, I started out running in lousy footwear. My first mistake was wearing tennis shoes. Think about it. Your feet are doing very different things on the tennis court: sidestepping, backpedaling, quick stopping, and lots of standing around. When you run, your feet are performing a single task, but doing it relentlessly. Shoes for these sports are correspondingly different. A good running shoe provides "support and cupping of the heel, firm arch support, protection of the ball of the foot, and flexibility of the front sole for easy push-off," according to Dr. Harry Hlavac, chief podiatrist of the Sports Clinic of the California College of Podiatric Medicine of San Francisco. All this can be accomplished in a shoe that will provide excellent traction; resist rain, snow, and winter salt compounds; and weigh no more than a feather. My second mistake was switching from tennis shoes to a cheap pair of running shoes that provided none of these features. They were lightweight by virtue of having nothing to them.

Each year, the October issue of *Runner's World* magazine (P.O. Box 366, Mountain View, California 94040) contains a consumer's guide to running shoes. Before you look for shoes, be sure also to read Chapter Four, which elaborates on feet and shoes. Then locate a good sports-shoe store. Talk to the salesmen. Bring or buy a pair of athletic socks. Then don't just try the shoes on. Ask to take a jog outside. Any good running-shoe salesman will encourage you to do so. If you are going to insert a special orthotic appliance, arch support, or other device, make sure you have it in there before trying the shoe. Nothing is more important for satisfying, healthy running or jogging than well-constructed, well-fitting shoes.

Put your money in good shoes, not in fancy warm-up suits. Regular runners and joggers are more likely to wear simple cotton or nylon shorts and T-shirts. Nylon is lighter and dries faster. When the weather gets nippy, you can gradually add sweat clothes. I run even at temperatures below zero and wind-chill factors of minus 70 degrees Fahrenheit. That ordeal calls for long johns, running shorts *and* sweat pants, a nylon windbreaker, wool hat, hooded sweat shirt, gloves, glove liners, and a ski mask or muffler that covers everything but the eyes.

Even with good weather, the perfect shoe, and the perfect course, you, like me, will spend some time on the injured list. Runners' complaints include blisters, muscle pulls, Achilles tendinitis, ankle sprains, sore knees, cramps, hamstring pulls, shinsplints, heel spurs, plantar fasciitis, and so on. Experienced runners use a combination of tape, Vaseline, and powder, while some go sockless and others chose theirs carefully—all to minimize blisters. Warm-up is most important. Stretching exercises or a slow first mile are prescribed by many doctors and coaches. Yoga has become a popular warm-up for runners; it tends to stretch the muscles that are shortened by running. Added flexibility reduces the risk of injury. Shirley MacLaine does both running and yoga.

Whatever happens, don't necessarily accept any one doctor's diagnosis. Get several opinions. If the prob-

lem involves the foot, try to find a sports-minded podiatrist. A famous orthopedic surgeon kept me in pain
for a year and did nothing to solve the problem that
my podiatrist treated and eliminated.

Before you start running, get checked by a doctor.
Ask for an exercise stress test, which involves an electrocardiogram administered while you run on a treadmill. Curiously, you may do better on the test before
you start your running program than later on. Heart
specialist Dr. George Sheehan finds that the results of
cardiac examinations performed on runners are often
wrongly interpreted by doctors who don't know anything about their special cardiovascular physiology. In
his excellent book, *Dr. Sheehan on Running*, he says
that runners have three natural enemies: dogs, drivers,
and doctors. To be sure, but I would go straight to
my doctor at the onset of any chest pain or the like.

I am chugging along against the wind, squinting
into the sun, now well above the lake. Were I returning from a twenty-mile run, I would be approaching
the "wall of pain" that runners talk about. This is the
point at which our stored energy, or glycogen, has
been depleted, and we continue only on will and de-
termination. Some claim to smash through it in the
last few miles of a marathon. I never have. Twenty
miles makes every joint and muscle hurt. I feel like a
ninety-year-old with arthritis. The twenty-mile mark,
it is said, is the halfway point in a twenty-six-mile
marathon.

But today I have only four or five miles behind me,
and the holistic stages of the run begin, called by
some, runner's "high." Unlike the second-wind theory,
which is supported by scientific data, I have only .
my own experience to offer about holistic running,
along with some exciting theoretical notions of people

like Professors Albert Szent-Gyoergyi and Carl Sagan, and some parallels with Zen and yoga. Feeling pretty good, I increase my pace a bit, knowing that I have only about four miles to go. My body is now a running machine—breath, stride, mind all focused on the run.

I look to the west and the cars appear to be floating above the road, like an endless flock of Canadian geese going home for the summer. A runner comes toward me. As he passes, we exchange power salutes. Much more passes between us than in pedestrians' encounters.

I sense why I am out here, suffering some, sweating lots, in rain, snow, wind, blazing sun, bitter cold, when I could be lots of other places, not the least of which is in bed. I *sense* the reasons, but they are not all easily articulated.

Of course, the first reason is health. The late Dr. Paul Dudley White said, "One can grow healthier as one grows older." A man of sixty running marathons, like Townes, is not uncommon. Joe Pardo is fifty-three and blind. He runs three times a day, a hundred miles per week. Virgil McIntyre is a record holder at age sixty-five. He runs even though he has a resectioned lung and a complicated hip ailment. D. B. Pettengill has run for nine years, after having a pneumonectomy. Jack Foster ran in the '76 Olympic marathon at age forty-four.

Dr. Morton Pastor started his seventy-one-year-old invalid mother jogging. She was taking half a dozen different medicines for congenitive heart failure, chronic arthritis, and other maladies. First he had her walking, then jogging fifteen seconds or so, followed by more walking. Soon she was jogging a half-hour per day. She stopped requiring medicines. She lost more than fifty pounds and seemed to be in significantly better health. By the time she was seventy-three, she had improved her health to a point where it was better than it had been in twenty years. She also started to dye her hair brown because she started going out with younger men.

As for myself, at thirty-eight, I am twenty pounds lighter than when I got my first driver's license at age sixteen. I feel better and stronger than ever. My pulse and probably my blood pressure are lower. I can better tolerate stressful problems in my office and elsewhere.

There is evidence that running lowers cholesterol levels. Research at Stanford University on middle-aged runners has shown that running increases high-density lipoprotein (HDL) levels in their blood. HDL's appear to protect people from heart disease by removing cholesterol from artery walls and preventing its deposit there. According to Dr. Peter Wood, " . . . the runners' plasma lipoprotein patterns might be mistaken for those typical of young women."

Vigorous exercise, time after time, has been found to reduce the risk of coronary disease. Dr. Thomas Bassler, editor of the *American Medical Joggers Association Bulletin*, claims that no marathoner of any age has ever had a fatal heart attack. There was one case of a death just last year that caused quite a stir among runners and joggers. Jim Shettler, a forty-two-year-old long-distance runner, died on an easy short run, the day after a twenty-three-mile run. He had run for twenty-five years and won the National AAU (American Athletic Union) Masters' twenty-five-kilometer event within a year of his death. Shettler ran ten miles a day. But Drs. Joan and Don Ullyot, both runners, performed an autopsy and concluded that the causes of cardiac failure related to his family history and to stress. His running, they concluded, probably *prolonged* his life.

Americans are beginning to understand that health is not bought from a doctor—at any price—but is acquired and maintained by virtue of luck, heredity, and life style. We can't do anything about the first two, but we can do plenty about the third. "The next major advances in the health of the American people," says Dr. John Knowles, president of the Rockefeller Foundation, "will result from the assumption of individual responsibility for one's own health."

However, the payoff in good health is not the only reason why so many of us are running. After all, Dr. Cooper's aerobic charts require a fraction of the mileage and speed that long-distance-running addicts demand. Running is a good way to control weight, but it is hardly cosmetics that keep me going. My wife, children, and friends have recently told me I look too thin. The definitive runner carries no more than two pounds of body weight for each inch of height. Have a good look at the faces and bodies of long-distance runners before or after a race, while they are in their skivvies. A bonier, more cadaverous throng of skeletons would be hard to find. No, the man or woman with a desire to beautify the body (and lots of money) would do better to build a swimming pool in a heated wing of the house.

Nor are runners usually driven by the American compulsion to beat out the competition at any cost. I've discovered that competition in running is very gentle, even among racers. People who bump into each other in the Boston marathon say, "Excuse me," and mean it. They help each other to cups of water along the way, or share them. Runners have been

known to cross the finish line simultaneously, holding
hands, to the consternation of AAU judges. The over-
whelming majority of runners have little need to race
in competition at all. When we race, it is the ritual
that draws us, not the prospect of winning. Our satisfactions are internal.

For if running and jogging have a therapeutic effect
on the body, they may have an even greater effect on
the soul. Several runners tell me that, for them, the alternative to running is psychoanalysis. Our running
begins to keep our bodies fit and to satisfy our need
for play, but it also progresses through stages of
deeper meaning, to expand our self-awareness, to become a holistic aspect of our lives. It is indeed a form
of worship, an attempt to find God, a means to the
transcendent. After forty-eight hours without a run, I
begin to fret and get testy with those around me. It is
more than a signal from my body that it wants something to do. "In pleasant ease and security, how soon
the soul begins to die," wrote Robinson Jeffers. I live
on the edge. I refuse to let flab and lassitude define
me. I have power, power that propels me cross country, puts me intimately in touch with nature,
strengthens my body, expands my mind. When I run,
my power is not destroying nature or manipulating
anyone else. It is transforming only me.

Within a mile from home, I put everything left into
a final "kick." My pace increases, my stride lengthens,
stretching the muscles in my calves and thighs. Breath
rushes in and out almost violently. I am overtaking
and passing early commuters waiting for buses and
trains. Their urban instincts cause them to wheel
around as I approach, some of them expecting to find
a slavering maniac descending upon them.

Finally, I finish in front of my house. My arms go

up high over my head, to lift my lungs and increase their capacity to gulp more air, but also to exalt the morning, the run, myself. The young delinquent in Alan Sillitoe's novella, *Loneliness of the Long-Distance Runner*, speaks for me: "Sometimes I think I've never been as free as during that couple of hours when I'm trotting up the path."

It is about 7:30 A.M. I have been up since before dawn. I have seen the world at its loveliest moment. I have run more than eight miles, made my body stronger, and enriched my soul. I will shave, have a hot shower that will seem exotic and sensual, eat, and be off to do what all of us do. The difference is—I own the day.

2

Work, Play, and Rest:
Fitting the Pieces Back Together

My object in living is to unite
My avocation and my vocation
As my two eyes make one in sight.
Only where love and need are one,
And the work is play for mortal stakes,
Is the deed ever really done
For Heaven and the future's sakes.
From "Two Tramps in Mudtime"
by ROBERT FROST

I shouldn't have been so angry when I saw the promotional blurb: four-day "running workshops" at the Princess Tower resort in the Bahamas. Labeled "Beyond Jogging," the "clinics" were to be conducted by staff of the Esalen Institute. I shouldn't have been so angry because the people conducting the workshop knew something about running and the vacationing seekers would be getting much more for their money than they would have gotten from other self-help courses. They would run, exercise, learn to breathe, perhaps get started on meditation—all authentic aspects of the running phenomenon. But it bothered me that running was yet another valid and beneficial activity that looked like it would end up in the hands of the "transcendental hucksters." These are the businessmen who rip off authentic religious, spiritual, and psychological movements and oversell them, promising easy ecstasy, blinding insights, total transformations, miracles. Ain't no miracles going to occur to those folks who fly down to the Bahamas for "Beyond Jogging." Blisters for sure, soreness very likely, better physical condition if they keep it up, but they are not going to find that their lousy marriages become idyllic and their boring jobs turn inspirational. Unreal expectations may arise. As a result, many people will try running and then quit when the sky doesn't open in the first month to reveal heaven.

Running is like yoga, meditation, and making love in this sense: It is an authentic way to approach the life beyond the one we experience through our five senses, but it is not a quick ticket to nirvana. Don't expect an overwhelmingly transcendent phenomenon that will make you a different person than you were before. "*Holos*" is a Greek word that means "entire." Holistic health, a new concept in medicine, means the integration of mind, body, and spirit for the attainment of whole health. This book represents the first attempt to explain and analyze an even newer concept: holistic running. Holistic running refers to the experience of long-distance running beyond what is required for *physical* fitness, as a means of helping to integrate our physical and spiritual selves; our work, play, and leisure; our relations to one another and the world. To accomplish this, holistic running incorporates aspects of exercise physiology along with Western religion, biochemistry, biofeedback, yoga, and Zen.

For me, holistic running—running beyond the threshold of fitness—has been a means of personal exploration. It has helped me encounter the dim, confusing isolation of my subjective self. It has taught me something about how I work, how the universe works, and how I fit in. And it continues to help me understand myself and the world. I'm learning about Nature and my own nature. I accomplish more than I ever did before, and I have greater inner strength. But none of this happened overnight. And I'm still essentially the same person I have always been.

So I begin my attempt to explain the phenomenon of holistic running by warning you that—while it is real and it *is* about more than improving your wind—it is not *everything*. I am awake seventeen or eighteen hours a day. I run an average of only one of those hours. Unless you are training for the Olympics, don't let running consume your waking hours! Your life may become a little livelier and a little deeper for your running. And running may even help to unclog one part of your life, because running is a powerful paradigm for many of life's activities; it reminds us that most things are accomplished only slowly and with effort, step by step. "Leg over leg the poodle dog went to Dublin," wrote James Joyce. But you must not expect miracles. No single activity, including running, can fulfill a person's life. As the splendid actor Bruce Dern, also a champion marathon runner, says, "If running is the only thing you have to look forward to, you can look at a calendar and predict somewhere along the line you're going to break down—either mentally, physically, or psychologically."

Having first issued this warning, in the next two chapters I will attempt to help you understand the running phenomenon and encourage you to experience it. This chapter relates running to the basic human activities of work, play, and rest, and then it focuses on more subjective characteristics of the phenomenon—how running seems to be able to change one's state of mind and even one's involuntary organic functions. Finally, a theory is offered to explain what goes on inside our bodies and our minds when we run long distances. In the next chapter, a simple program is laid out in order to make holistic running a part of your life.

Running as Work

When I first wrote about running, many people commented on the extraordinary "discipline" I demonstrated by hauling myself out of the house before dawn and doing six or eight miles. I was dumbfounded. To me, discipline meant Marine boot camp or breaking rocks in a prison compound. Those are work, drudgery. But running is a delight. "How earnest you are," they would add, "to run in such bad weather." Again I was surprised. How awful it would be to stay *in* just because of the weather.

On reflection, I understand that there is a connection between running and such Prussian qualities as discipline and character. I run for pleasure and to expand my awareness, but there is, nevertheless, a definite link between running and the positive attributes of solid work. In earlier times, most people were workers in the traditional sense: They hunted, fought, farmed, built, or wove. The privileged did not have to work to survive, but found that they needed work to live. England's Edwardian elite adopted such rigors as the fox hunt. Many pampered children of the rich still muck out stables, clean tack, groom and ride horses as if their lives depended on it—and in a sense, they do.

Konstantin Levin, in Tolstoy's *Anna Karenina*, was irresistibly compelled to be active, and he especially liked mowing, an activity not generally engaged in by rich, educated landowners. "I must have physical exercise, or my temper'll certainly be ruined," he told his brother. "Really! what an idea! But tell me," his brother responded, "how do the peasants look at it? I suppose they laugh in their sleeves at their master's being such a queer fish?" Levin's satisfaction from mowing was very great:

> Levin walked back . . . along his own swath. Though the sweat was pouring down his face and dripping from his nose and his back was as wet as if it had been soaked in water, he felt happy. What pleased him particularly was that now he knew that he would be able to hold out . . .

> Suddenly, without knowing what it was or whence it came, he became conscious in the middle of his work of a pleasant sensation of coolness on his hot, perspiring shoulders . . .

> Levin lost all consciousness of time and had no idea whatever whether it was late or early. His work was undergoing a change which gave him intense pleasure. There were moments in the middle of his work when he forgot what he was doing, he felt quite at ease.

This almost mystical need for hard physical toil has been established not only by psychologists, but by physical scientists as well. "Entropy" is the scientific term used to describe the tendency of organized forms to disintegrate gradually. "Syntropy," is the tendency of organized forms to reach higher and higher levels of harmony and order. Buckminster Fuller believes there is conflict between the two principles and that the final victory of syntropy is the noblest work of man. "My continuing philosophy," he wrote, "is predicated on the assumption that in dynamic counterbalance to the expanding universe of entropically increasing random disorderliness there must be a universal pattern of omni-contracting, convergent, progressive orderliness and that man is that anti-entropic reordering function."*

Entropy results in death, syntropy in life. The Nobel Prize-winning scientist Albert Szent-Gyoergyi says that the "drive" to syntropy is the compulsion of living matter to perfect itself. According to Szent-Gyoergyi, scientists can show that the heart that fails and causes death has behaved like a heart that rested *too much*. The heart is at its strongest when it has rested the minimum, not the maximum, interval. "Life keeps life going," says Szent-Gyoergyi, "building up and improving itself, while inactivity makes it go to pieces." If our hearts work too little, if our legs are not used enough, they atrophy.

Professor Szent-Gyoergyi tries to explain in scientific terms how Konstantin Levin can develop *more* energy through hard work than he expends, and *enjoy* it to the extent that he does not consider it work. The key, he says is "charge-transfer energy." An electron of a molecule (A) can go over to another molecule (B), if they are in very intimate contact. This happens in order to stabilize the system, as a boulder that is pried up then rolls downhill, or when a magnet attracts a piece of iron. Potential energy becomes kinetic energy as the two elements move toward each other. When the two elements again come to rest, the kinetic energy is released and can be utilized to do useful work. This is "charge-transfer" energy. The "charge-transfer energy" contributes to the forces keeping the system stable. Without it, the system would more likely go to pieces.

* From Szent-Gyoergyi, "Drive in Living Matter to Perfect Itself." Synthesis, Vol. 1, No. 1 (1976).

The same sort of process occurs inside us, says Szent-Gyoergyi, when—as a result of effort—we mow acres of crops or run eight miles or overcome a challenge of a similar energy-expending kind. We supply the initial energy that allows some of our personality elements to move closer together and form a more harmonious structure. This psychological synthesis results in a new energy, a feeling that can be described as an "urge to action." Energy begets energy, work begets work.

The problem is that today most people have difficulty finding the kind of work that gets those electrons flowing. Most of our nine-to-five jobs require virtually no physical challenge and, all too often, no serious intellectual challenge either. In fact, we were never taught that hard work is good for us. We were unwittingly led into a state of entropy.

When I was a kid, I was conscientiously kept from the challenges of hard work, first by a father who loved well, but not very wisely, and then by a school system designed, as the former Yale chaplin William Sloan Coffin says, "more for gain than for growth." In the evening, my father and I would begin an elaborate project with my Erector set. Bedtime would come for me long before the project was completed. Invariably, when I got up in the morning, it would be like Christmas: In the living room I would find a motorized Ferris wheel, or an operating crane, or some other fully achieved project that had been lovingly finished by my father while I slept. All *I* had to do was press a button and make it work. He loved me so much he wrote my speeches, built my model airplanes, and buffered me in so many other ways from engagement with the world.

Nor did I learn anything about the real rewards of

work in that gargantuan institution of entropy, school. "If you would learn to defraud the consumer, observe the educators," says Dr. Sheehan. "They imprison their audiences; set up delusionary goals called success and happiness; sell inadequate means called science and the humanities; and disparage their competitors, the body and the spirit." Good grades seemed to be a function of mastering gimmicks, not concepts or subjects. I succeeded by raising my hand a lot, offering glib answers to facile questions, providing the expected on exams, playing the teachers' games. I spent many gym periods thumbing through idiotic magazines in the nurse's office on contrived but acceptable medical excuses, insulated from the challenge to climb further up the rope, or swim more laps than I could do with ease. Ease, not work, was the name of the game. In fact it was—and is—entropy.

There was one momentary aberration during my sophomore year when, very briefly, I volunteered for the wrestling team—not out of interest in the sport or in the condition of my body, but because I wanted a school "letter" to sew on my jacket, a symbol that was highly valued by others. I chose wrestling, thinking that my weight category might offer an easy opportunity to earn the letter with the same ease as I earned good grades. This interlude lasted two days. The first day we were ordered onto the track for a one-mile run and warned that this would be a regular part of each day's training. I was not only exhausted by the effort, but offended at being asked to do something so apparently unrelated to the sport of wrestling. The second day did me in altogether. Far from being the only volunteer in the 115–120 pound class, I found myself working out against a cheerful, wiry, fast, and incredibly strong kid, Donald Hubbard. He was terrific. My career as an interscholastic athlete was over.

For at least a few others, though, school sports—particularly running—can be the first authentic experience of work, or syntropy. Jamie Kalven remembers his discovery of running when he tried out for the high school track team. "It was the first thing in my life that I *really* did, where I made the full effort, devoted myself overtime to the discipline." Kalven who is now close to thirty, put aside his "career" as a runner in college. "But the metaphor still has resonance," he adds. "Running is a reminder of something important for me—of how you do things, of how to muster your capacities for the full effect." Now a writer, he finds that the best way to overcome a writer's block is to go out for a run.

Bruce Dern had a similar experience. "The reason I ran, [in high school and college], more than any other, is because it is the purest form of honesty that there is. You have point X and you have another point Y, and you go from here to there. The watch doesn't lie . . . and there's no bullshit. There's no cheating."

To make it on the high school track or playing field, as Kalven and Dern did, requires real effort, hundreds of hours of training, the sacrifice of more immediate gratifications. Many of us are sensitive to the soul-shriveling results of invidious competition, too often the obsession of coaches and parents, but what else as authentic and satisfying is available to the kid in a modern American school?

In my case, the lessons about work that Kalven and Dern learned on the high school track continued to evade me through Harvard College. Harvard had changed little since Henry Adams's undergraduate experience in the 1850s. "The entire work of the four years," he said, "could have been easily put into the work of any four months in afterlife." "Work" wasn't required. The college didn't promise that every certified graduate had worked hard to earn his degree. It has always been a "mild and liberal school," as Adams called it, believing that its students are fairly bright and interesting upon admission, and offering them decent access to some intelligent, witty professors as well as a colossal collection of books. The result was that one could achieve a certain "style" there, not an insignificant gift and not a common one in America. Adams called this gift "self-possession." He said that "self-possession was the strongest part of Harvard College, which certainly taught me to stand alone."

But too often self-possession also provides an additional means of succeeding without experiencing hard work. At least it did for me. Only after I completed school, including law school, did I finally discover the satisfactions of unrelenting, consuming, painfully hard work. Running was the original paradigm of syntropy for Kalven. For me, it was the opposite: The energy I finally generated by practicing my crafts as a lawyer and a writer stimulated me to begin running as recreation. The system of molecules A and B tends to add further molecules, and so become more stable, better, and more complex. By working, we finally arrive at a "drive" to improvement. Work begets play, play begets work. Running for me was begat by work, and so some would call it "play," but the term is somewhat deceptive, as we shall see.

Running as Play

Look back at Robert Frost's verse that introduces

this chapter. In the poem, Frost is chopping wood on his farm when two hungry hoboes arrive and offer to do the "work" for a fee. Frost, of course, says no:

> Only where love and need are one,
> And the work is play for mortal stakes,
> Is the deed ever really done
> For Heaven and the future's sakes.

It is hard to distinguish between the work and play of the healthy person, although we often try. Holistic running can't be characterized as *all* work or *all* play. which is why I'm always surprised when someone compliments me on the discipline I demonstrate by early-morning workouts; they are perceiving the effort as work, while I see it, as Frost saw his chopping, as a holistic element of life. On the other hand, some people dismiss holistic running as too playful to be an important part of the life of a grown-up—a point of view that also overlooks the whole.

What Frost says with such economy is that his vocation, poetry, is abstract and of the mind, like many others. Yet we are also creatures of the flesh, with bodies as well as minds that must be exercised. The farmer, the mother, the athlete, have the advantage over us white-collar types. They are more likely to combine work and play, to make the abstract concrete in their everyday lives. Other "simpler" cultures don't have the problem of separating work and play. A marvelous little book, *Letter to Teacher*, written by Italian peasant boys who formed an alternative school when they flunked out of the state schools, forcefully makes the point that modern man suffers for separating work and play:

At the gymnastics exam the teacher threw us a ball and said, "Play basketball." We didn't know how. The teacher looked us over with contempt: "My poor children."

He too is one of you. The ability to handle a conventional ritual seemed so vital to him. He told the principal that we had not been given any "physical education" and we should repeat the exams in the fall.

Any one of us could climb an oak tree. Once up there we could let go with our hands and chop off a two-hundred-pound branch with a hatchet. Then we could drag it through the snow to our mother's doorstep.

I heard of a gentleman in Florence who rides upstairs in his house in an elevator. But then he has bought himself an expensive gadget and pretends to row in it. You would give him an A in Physical Education.

Unity of work and play was part of Indian culture as well. In "Childhood in an Indian Village," Wilfred Pelletier, a young Odawa Indian, describes the people's attitude in the village of Wikwemikong on Ontario's Manitaulin Island, where he grew up:

And just as we didn't separate our learning from our way of life, we didn't separate our work from it either. The older women, for example, who used to work all day at whatever—tanning hides, etc.—didn't really think of it as work. It was a way of life. That's the real difference between the kind of society we have now where we equate these kinds of things with work and yet will go out and play sports and enjoy it, and the kind of society I'm talking about. Here, we go and work and use maybe half or a quarter of the energy we spend playing sports, but we call it work and we feel differently about it altogether. These are the kinds of differences that exist. Indian people who had a way of life and who felt it was their way of life didn't call it work. It was part of the way they provided for their families; and they "worked" very hard.

Holistic running is not the only physical activity that can help reintegrate our lives. But it is an especially good one because it involves very little in the way of abstract rules, rigid schedules, or point-by-point competition. It is almost pure play in the classic sense. In contrast, think about tennis. The preliminary warm-up before a tennis match is hardly what motivates most tennis players. They are there for the contest, the competition. But the holistic runner is out there almost every time for the workout alone. What are considered in most sports only preliminaries to be hurried through are the very essence of running, possibly the only popular athletic activity in America in which the process is more rewarding than the goal. In holistic running, as Gandhi said about life, "the means are the ends in process."

Dr. Sheehan calls his running play: "And in that hour of play I discovered, or rediscovered, myself. Finally I accepted the person I was." Used in this sense, play begins to carry a mystical, or religious, meaning. And rightly so.

Running as Rest

After work and play, the next basic element of human activity is rest. If work is creation and play is recreation, rest is re-creation, the time for affirming, consolidating, and renewing. There has traditionally been a religious aspect to the notion of rest. In his recent book, *Turning East: The Promise and the Peril of the New Orientalism,* Professor Harvey Cox of the Harvard Divinity School explains that "Sabbath" in

Hebrew comes from a root that means "to desist." Sabbath, he says, was originally a time set aside for ceasing all activities and acknowledging the goodness of creation. The Bible reports many occasions when Jesus took time out to withdraw and be alone. St. John Climacus of the early Eastern Church taught a form of meditation that involved concentrating on each breath, using the name of Jesus as a kind of mantra. Later teachers in this tradition taught disciples to attach a prayer to each breath and to focus their attention on the centers of their own bodies while meditating, striving to see the inner light of the Transfiguration.

The ability to rest in this rather profound sense, I think, depends on one's ability to work in an equally profound way—not to slide through a day at the office, but to come away with a sense that your work has achieved some creative result. God worked for six days to create the world. On the seventh, He deserved and took a rest. Professor Cox tells us that the word "rest" literally means "to catch one's breath."

For Oriental masters, the deep harmonies of meditation, or ultimate rest, are the key to all of life. As with the Odawa Indians of Canada, no boundaries divide the Oriental life of work and play from the spiritual one of ultimate rest. For the most devout, total transience, total stillness, a state of outer and inner rest are the goals. But we in the West continue to cope with a culture that separates work, play, and rest.

I don't lament the loss of total transience or total stillness, for work is essential to me, as it is to the Western God. But work alone is not enough. I must catch my breath. Breath is a source of replenishment, of renewal, of re-creation. If work is creation, the

Sabbath, the period of anti-work, the catching of one's breath, is re-creation. Creation and re-creation are essential if the cycle is to be repeated.

Just as holistic running involves elements of work and play, it also involves elements of rest. In a sense, running is my Sabbath. When I run, I cannot think about the sticky complexities of my professional work because such thoughts knot me up and slow me down. The Bible says that on the Sabbath King David danced and leaped before the ark. Not much separates King David's ritual from mine. True to the Sabbath tradition, on my run I can contemplate the work of God, see the dawn slowly give color to nature, feel the sun, the wind, the gentle texture of the earth, the uncompromising concrete we have laid on top of it. I am caught up in my breath and my body, sensitive to my heart and my limbs, at one with the world of God's creation, not manipulating or destroying it, just a part of it. The Buddhists call this form of consciousness *sati*, the "bare awareness" that is a goal of meditation—achieving a consciousness of the world, but having no designs on it.

Running Through Mind and Body

Running can help to unify the objective world of action, and it seems to have a similar effect on the subjective world of mind and body. There is evidence to suggest that holistic running can change your state of mind, and that your state of mind can influence the rhythms of organic activity within your body.

A 1973 Purdue University study by Professors Ismail and Trachtman, published in *Psychology Today*, asserts that the brain functions more imaginatively and thoughtfully in a physically fit person, for two reasons. First, blood circulation is improved, which provides the brain with more biochemical nutrients, especially glycogen, a form of energy derived from carbohydrates. And second, the athlete's psychological health improves. Each time he exercises, the athlete confronts a psychologically difficult challenge and demands that his body overcome it. He is rewarded with a sense of accomplishment, independence, and control over his own life that he may never have felt before. Ismail and Trachtman found that after going through a rigorous schedule of running and other exercises, their subjects were less given to hypochondriacal complaining, and were more extroverted and self-confident. Middle-aged men, the doctors said, were "likely to become more self-sufficient, resolute, emotionally stable and imaginative" when they became physically fit.

The mind apparently can reciprocate for these benefits conferred on it by the body. Physical performance can be enhanced by what the writer Adam Smith calls "powers of mind." Total concentration, total attention, are the rewards. San Francisco 49er's quarterback John Brodie told Smith that "an intention carries a force, a thought connected with an energy that can stretch itself out in a pass play or a golf shot, or a base hit, or a thirty-five-foot jump shot in basketball." Brodie's concentration appears to slow down the action of the defensive lineman moving in on him, giving him more time to get the pass away, "like a movie or a dance in slow motion. It's beautiful."

Running can help some people make even deeper connections between body and mind. While we focus our conscious efforts on relaxing our bodies to achieve maximum performance at an efficient level of operation, the so-called involuntary rhythms of the body can also be controlled by the process of biofeedback. Basically, the concept of biofeedback involves putting a person in a closed feedback loop in which information concerning one or more of his bodily functions is continually reported to him. Biofeedback researchers say that when a person has that information, he can learn, more or less, to control the bodily functions involved.

A runner's control of his breathing is one form of biofeedback, and so is his ability to sense which of his muscles are tight and to relax them. But now there is evidence that runners can do much more than this to control their bodies. In 1977, two doctors, Goldstein and Brady, published the results of their study, "Biofeedback Heart Rate Training During Exercise," in which runners were hooked up to biofeedback machines while they ran on treadmills. The machines reported their heart rates back to them. They could breathe any way they wished; they could tense or relax their muscles; they could think any thoughts that they pleased, as long as they lowered their heart rates. They were not told told how to do this. At the end of five weeks and twenty-five sessions, the mean heart rate of the group had gone down about 10 percent more than that of the control group. How did they do it? According to an analysis of the results, some reported success by changing their breathing patterns, others thought "relaxed thoughts," while still others went into a trance or concentrated on objects around them.

The doctors concluded that "*no technique* reliably related to performance." In other words, there is no specific step-by-step process. Biofeedback seems to be a means of breaking down the barriers between our conscious and subconscious, between our minds and bodies. Once we can do that, the results apparently flow as naturally as when we command our eyelids to close or our feet to walk. When the doctors took the successful subjects off the biofeedback machines, they continued to be able to lower their heart rates at will. The machines, it seems, had merely introduced their consciousness to their subconsciousness, and that was all that was needed. When I run, I carry my own biofeedback machine. Going beyond the fifth mile, I can tune in to the rhythms of my heart and my lungs. I *will* my body to work well, to relax, to run efficiently—and it does.

How Holistic Running Works: A Theory

Many people care about running for exercise and fitness. They seek nothing more. They discover nothing more. Fine. Holistic running is different though. It is not work, nor play, nor rest, but all three of these. It has an impact on our minds and spirits as well as our bodies.

It may seem outrageous for a lay person with no medical or scientific training to attempt an explanation of holistic running. I haven't partaken of any of the human potential programs. I haven't been through formal courses in transcendental meditation, yoga, group therapy, or Rolfing. I have never even been trained as a runner. Nevertheless, there may be enough experience and information available in the work of experts for me to synthesize a theory of what is happening to me, and to outline a simple means to enable you to try it too.

Knob Knowledge: We Don't Know What We Think We Know

A new television set is delivered to your house. Your four-year-old daughter watches you take it out of the box, place it on a table, hook up the antenna, and plug in the electrical cord. She examines it for a while, fiddles with the knobs. She turns a knob and the picture appears. It works! She can make the TV set work, but she doesn't know *how* it works. Precocious four-year-old that she is, she will not agree. She thinks she knows the TV set—and she certainly knows all she needs to know to make it work. She has knob knowledge of the TV set.

Similarly, fitness runners who put in their five-day-a-week forty-minute jog in fulfillment of Dr. Kenneth Cooper's minimum aerobics requirements will not agree that there is much more to know about running. In fact they already know all they need to know.

This chapter is written for those who believe that there is more to understanding ourselves than the equivalent of knob knowledge and that holistic running may provide one means to this deeper understanding. Our exploration begins with scientific speculation about the evolution of the human brain and how it relates to the evolution of human consciousness in Zen and yoga psychology.

Running Through the Brain's Evolution

Research on animals and humans indicates that blood flow to the brain is increased 20 percent by strenuous exercise such as running. This was one of the findings of the Ismail and Trachtman study of the psychology of runners discussed earlier in this chapter. Abundant medical evidence links the available blood supply and the functioning of the brain. If the brain is deprived of oxygen for a few minutes, serious and permanent mental disability may result. On the other hand, when a surgeon has removed material obstructing clogged carotid arteries to minimize risk of stroke, the patient's IQ has shot up substantially, by as much as eighteen points. Another example of the same principle: some medical authorities speculate that infants who have been treated with hyperbaric oxygen—oxygen under high pressure—can become more intelligent.

Common sense tells us, then, that compared to the measures just described, the effect of a brief sprint on the brain's blood supply is insignificant, while an aerobic jog of thirty minutes probably has only moderate effect. So it is no wonder that those who have tried jogging or running and quit before they were able to run more than a mile or two tend to scorn the idea that more is involved than a mere workout. Fitness runners who keep it up, but stay at the forty-minute five-times-a-week level recommended by Dr. Cooper, are also likely to remain skeptical that their consciousness might expand with longer runs. Yet, if we look at more speculative ideas about how the brain functions, we can get an idea why higher levels of experience through holistic running can *only* be reached at longer distances.

In his extraordinary book, *The Dragons of Eden*, Carl Sagan never mentions running or other forms of exercise, but he offers a model of the human brain that I have found very helpful in this inquiry. The human brain is "triune," he says—that is, it has three parts. For some activities, such as sex, Sagan thinks that all parts of the brain are simultaneously engaged, but for others, perhaps including running, the parts of the brain may be involved sequentially.

The oldest and most primitive part of the brain, according to Sagan, is the R-complex, which we share with fish and reptiles. It controls the heart, blood, circulation, respiration, and provides us with an essential for self-preservation: the ability to get out of danger fast—the ability to run. The R-complex appears to influence the ritualistic and hierarchical aspects of our lives, and it is this part of the brain that the sprinters and devotees of aerobics are engaging when they run—this primitive part, but no more.

The limbic system of the brain surrounding the R-complex is something fish and reptiles don't have. By controlling the thalamus, hypothalamus, and pituitary functions, it seems to generate vivid emotions. Strong mood alterations result from the activity of the pituitary gland. Electrical discharges in the limbic system give rise to "feelings" like those experienced on a drug-induced psychedelic trip. Sagan thinks that the limbic system may also be responsible for our sense of exhilaration and awe, and the more subtle emotions we think of as uniquely human. Recall the emotional high that Konstantin Levin achieved mowing the fields with his peasants. Look at a similar passage from *Four-Minute Mile*, a nonfiction book written by Roger Bannister, the first man to break the four-minute mile:

> Soon I was running across the moor to a distant part of the coast of Kintyre. It was near evening and fiery sun clouds were chasing over to Arron. It began to rain, and the sun shining brightly behind me cast a rainbow ahead. It gave me the feeling that I was cradled in the rainbow arc as I ran.

Perhaps these emotional rewards of exercise in general, and running in particular, come only when the increased blood flow has stimulated the limbic system to join the simpler R-complex in the brain's activity. If we accept this notion, we runners can begin to understand our own experiences as we run through the second- and third-wind stages, and nonrunners can begin to believe the ecstatic reports of those who have done it.

The third part of the brain, the neocortex, is the most advanced—and the most uniquely human, Sagan tells us. Humans have the most developed neocortex. In its lobes reside our capacities to reason, to regulate action, to associate abstractly, to remember, to anticipate the future, to worry, perhaps to feel satisfaction. The final stages of long-distance running, when it becomes holistic, may bring levels of insight and self-awareness that are undoubtedly beyond the reach of the lower mammals, and, in fact, seem to be attained by only a small portion of the human species—those who are willing to pay the price, like serious students of Zen and yoga, as well as long-distance runners. One of the other principal functions of the neocortex is to provide us with vision, the dominant sense in humans and other primates. Most runners (including this one) agree that they are less likely to reach their deepest levels of consciousness when they run at night, perhaps because they are inhibiting the fullest participation of the neocortex.

The human brain evolved from the reptilian brain, an evolution that may be recapitulated in life processes, such as in the development of the human embryo. This process is described in the common scientific phase "ontogeny (individual life cycle) recapitulates phylogeny (evolution of the race)."

Perhaps a similar kind of psychic recapitulation occurs during a long-distance run. We begin to run as a dinosaur or a lizard may have, for self-preservation. We must be fit to escape our enemies and to maintain the health of our basic body parts—the heart, lungs, and limbs. But remember what happened to the dinosaur. So we go on, to achieve second and third wind. Our limbic system is now engaged and we have recapitulated our evolution to the state of, say, the puma—loping through the high grass at the forest's edge. Finally, we reach our highest, our truly human, level, at which thoughts and insights bring us to the edge of unique human awareness—what some might call a state of bliss.

Other thinkers have developed conceptual schemes similar to Sagan's, which also help in the search for an explanation of holistic running. For example, according to Plato, there are three stages, or degrees, or knowledge. The first and lowest, which the fish, reptile, and dinosaur shared with us, involves simple observation. We know, however, from physics, astronomy, chemistry, and good sense, that what you see is *not* what you get. (Remember the difference between knob knowledge of the TV set and real knowledge of its workings.) The second stage of knowledge unites simple observation and an "extrasensory" intelligence. It informs us, for instance, that the movement of the sun, moon, and stars we observe in the sky is not arbitrary, but subject to some system. But just like the intermediate operations of the limbic system provide us with feelings without deep understanding of our place in the scheme of things, Plato's second stage of knowledge does not provide man with the wisdom to understand the holistic connections between himself and the movement of the stars. It is Plato's third and highest stage, proper knowledge, which is wholly extrasensory, that does this. This knowledge, which comes only through pure perception of divine ideas, of the Supreme God, the Infinite, places man within the universe.

Plato's paradigm is not considered a scientific rendering of the human mind, and Sagan's has already been subject to attack. But, like other human representations of matters beyond our complete understanding, each may help us to a better understanding.

Split-Brain Theory

Another set of distinctions concerning the neocortex of the brain may also help. Researchers tell us that the neocortex is divided into a left and right hemisphere, each with separate functions and each controlling the opposite side of the body. The left hemisphere oversees the verbal, rational, practical functions—the most recent evolutionary developments of the human brain. The intuitive functions—spatial understanding, musical ability, dreaming, and other human functions that go much further back in our evolutionary history—are governed by the right hemisphere. A number of applications of this distinction suggest themselves. For example, I suppose that artists operate mainly out of their right neocortex hemisphere, critics out of the left. School children say, "I know the answer, but I can't explain it." If they are not fibbing, they mean that their right, or intuitive, hemisphere is more highly developed than their left, or verbal, one. Einstein said that he would get an idea, then later try to express it in words—meaning that he would try to verbalize with his left hemisphere the intuition that first occurred in his right hemisphere.

Because Western man tends to be dominated by his left hemisphere, he is rational, and he therefore realizes the importance of staying in good physical condition. But he frankly finds running a bore. It is repetitive, and not intellectually or even physically complex or challenging. It is not dependent on understanding oceanography, math, and astronomy, like sailing, which is considered an "intellectual" sport. Unlike scuba diving or auto racing, it is not dependent on technology. Western man is frustrated because running seems to keep his clear logical mind from operating at its most efficient level. This is confirmed in the ancient yoga text, *Swar Swarodayam*:

> In all harsh acts, in the reading and teaching of difficult sciences . . . in hunting . . . in climbing a high place or mountain, in gambling . . . in the breaking of . . . a horse . . . in athletic sports . . . in practising with swords, in battle, in eating . . . in harsh and hot deeds,

the right side of the body (the left hemisphere) is dominant. So the runner who perceives his running as "a harsh act" or "an athletic sport" or work, pure and simple, is not likely to achieve much beyond fitness from it.

The holistic runner wishes to give at least temporary dominance to his right hemisphere. Long-distance running is not a "harsh act" to him. He likes the smells, the sounds, the images of the run. He enjoys the simple, easy rhythms. He is happy to be lonely, in a pursuit where little verbalizing is possible. Notions, as they come to him and pass through his mind, never achieve the status of coherent, rational ideas. He is pleased to occupy his mind with dreamlike pictures, knowing that complex, logical thoughts can't be sustained while he runs at his best.

The holistic runner is stimulating his right brain. He experiences a primitive, sensual world, temporarily repressing his verbal, rational, modern self. He is the hunter again, as he was a million years ago, as he was for most of human history. He is recreating the childhood of mankind. Of course, he is not entirely governed by the right half of his neocortex. He can observe his primitive pleasures, appreciate them in themselves and as they are recorded by the temporarily repressed, but not altogether inactive, left hemisphere. As in a dream or a controlled drug trip, he "knows" where he is and that he can control the experience—come back from it when he has had enough. Unlike the person having a nightmare or bad trip, the runner doesn't risk losing control—not being able to return.

Zen and Yoga: The Psychology of the Right Brain

We can look East, to Zen and the Indian yoga tradition, for a means of using these essentially Western ideas linking mental states and physical sensations in such daily pursuits as running workouts. According to the scholar D. T. Suzuki, in Zen, disciplines as different as flower arranging, archery, and running "are not intended for utilitarian purposes only or for purely aesthetic enjoyments, but are meant to train the mind; indeed, to bring it into contact with the ultimate reality." An example of this process can be found in the extraordinary little book, *Zen in the Art of Archery*, by

Herrigel. He writes that the Zen master of archery advises:

> When drawing the string you should not exert the full strength of your body, but learn to let only your two hands do the work, while your arm and shoulder muscles remain relaxed, as though they have fulfilled one of the conditions that make drawing and shooting spiritual.

Yoga has been defined as "equanimity," or "efficiency in action," or "stoppage of the waves of the mind." Its concern is with a relationship between body and mind in which the two communicate intimately and are responsive to one another. It is one of the oldest disciplines that involve physical and mental control, and the deliberate induction of altered states of consciousness. Watch a person perform a series of yogic asanas or postures and all that you see is the extraordinary dexterity of his or her body and when you watch a long-distance runner, again, it seems that the process is entirely physical. But in fact, both practices can involve the full employment of mind and emotions, too, heightening one's awareness and clarifying one's relationship to the world. Yogic breathing and meditational techniques seem less "physical," more a matter of mind than body. Yet they result in startling changes in body functions, which have been measured and recorded in scientific studies using biofeedback and electrocardiograph machines.

Yoga is generally equated with the postures, or asanas, of hatha yoga, but there are several other forms of the discipline, such as the religious or devotional (bhakti), the service or action (karma), and the philosophical (jnana). Yoga can be translated as "path," and, as the yoga scholar Ramamurthi says,

"All paths converge toward the ultimate goal." Raja yoga, or the royal path, which was codified over a thousand years ago by Patañjali in the *Yoga Sutras*, involves a number of steps that begin with the body, then affect the breath, and finally, the mind. An Indian monk, Swami Rama, and two Americans, Rudolph Ballentine and Allan Weinstock (Swami Ajaya), have attempted to combine raja yoga with some fundamental aspects of Western medicine and psychology in their Himalayan Institute near Chicago, where they work with patients who in many cases have not responded to conventional Western therapies. Their work at the institute and their book *Yoga and Psychotherapy*, as well as Herrigel's *Zen in the Art of Archery*, have helped me design the six-step program presented in the next chapter. The program begins by dealing first with the basic physical workings of the body and then concludes with higher levels of spiritual awareness.

3

Holistic Running: A Six-Step Program

> The earth and myself are of one mind.
> The measure of the land and the measure
> Of our bodies are the same.
> *Chief Joseph of the Nez Percé Indians*

Deep inside the human body are systems that respond to such practices as religious ritual, meditation, and long-distance running. Through long-distance or holistic running, many of us have begun to get in touch with these inner systems, and to make connections between mind, body, and spirit. Holistic running also helps us tighten the connections between ourselves and the external world—connections we can sense and those remaining beyond the reach of our senses.

The six-step program of holistic running assumes that you are in good physical condition. If you are new to running, you should first read Chapters Four and Five, which deal with the prosaic but essential matters of physical health, including care of your feet and legs, the choice of good running shoes, the need for additional exercises, nutrition, and the importance of exercise stress tests if you are nearing thirty-five or forty years of age or have reason to doubt your health. Those who are already running may want to get in closer touch with their bodies by beginning with the early stages before they attempt to move up through the higher rungs of awareness.

Step 1: The Body

Begin by alternating walking and jogging until you are winded. Try walking a hundred yards, jogging the same distance, and so on for a mile. After a couple of weeks, see if you can jog a full mile. Do not worry about your speed. Let your body tell you if it is able to do more. Remember that physical fitness is essential, but you are also training your body for "higher" levels of functioning.

As you walk and jog, sense out areas of tenseness. Are you holding your shoulders unnaturally high? Are you hunched forward instead of erect? Concentrate on relaxing your muscles. Begin with the tips of your toes and gradually work upward. Make sure that your elbows and wrists are loose enough to work with the stride of your feet and legs. Try to maintain a smooth and regular pace, something that can only be done if you are relaxed.

Gradually you will find that you are running more and walking less. And what is more important, you will be aware of an increasing ability to relax and concentrate on your body. Later, this power of concentration will have enormous impact on your mind as well. Remember that this phase of your running program is so basic than even a dinosaur would be capable of accomplishing it. Only the primitive R-complex of your brain is involved, governing capabilities shared by virtually all creatures. "Tune in" on the basic functions brought into play. Feel your heart beat, listen to the rhythm of your feet. Do not ignore signals from your body that tell you it is time to slow down or stop.

Yogis, along with Western doctors, believe the body harbors various kinds of pollutants, such as metabolic byproducts and ingested chemicals, which impair good health and mental clarity. These pollutants are eliminated not only through excretion of the feces and urine but also through perspiration and breathing. As your running improves, feel the sweat rise to your skin and carry off the poisons. Help your lungs eliminate carbon dioxide by pushing your diaphragm and belly out as you inhale, then relaxing to let the fresh air refill your lungs.

Now we begin to transcend the Western dichotomy between reason and emotion. We sense that we can regulate parts of our bodies previously thought beyond voluntary control. The premise of biofeedback is that just as responses of our skeletal muscles are voluntary, so too, glandular and visceral response are voluntary. This does not seem farfetched anymore. Concentrate on your heart, your muscles, your nerves. Yogis can greatly alter their heart rates, but remember that American middle-aged runners have also done so consciously, through biofeedback techniques. Yogis have been known to have extremely high thresholds of pain, partly as a result of their ability to concentrate intently and manipulate bodily function. Studies by the American Medical Joggers Association now underway testing the pain thresholds of marathon runners, which are thought to be higher than average, may confirm the suspicion of some researchers that long-distance running modifies the pain threshold, just as yoga seems to do. But biofeedback should not be attempted without a more complete awareness of how these basic functions interact with other body systems and with the mind. So let us expand our awareness by advancing to the next stage of holistic running, in which we begin to integrate our breath, or energy (what in yoga is called "prana") with these other bodily functions.

Step 2: Breath

You have been running for at least eight to ten weeks now, and find that you can sustain a pace of ten minutes per mile for at least three or four miles without stopping. You have come a long way toward bringing your body under control, but you may find that now you are having trouble with the rhythm of your breathing. Be aware of your breathing. Simple awareness may correct many irregular breathing patterns. As your breathing becomes more regular, your running will improve, you will be calmer, you will go farther and faster. Mastery of the breath is the critical divide between those who will remain fitness runners (or drop out altogether) and those who may achieve holistic running.

The various levels of human functioning are called "sheaths" in the Taittiriya Upanishad. The most elementary sheath is the body, or the physical sheath, which we discussed above. The next sheath, called "the energy sheath" and consisting of breath, is encased in the physical sheath and has the same form. From this sheath, says the Taittiriya Upanishad, "man and beasts derive their life. For breath is the life of beings."

Breath—the intermediary between body and soul—is the key. *The Oxford English Dictionary* defines "psyche" as "breath, to breathe, to blow, hence life . . . the animating principle in man . . . the source of all vital activities, rational or irrational." The Hebrew representation of the name of God is only a slight modification of the Hebrew word "to be," which also signifies "to breathe." In the early Egyptian languages, *ka* meant the personal soul, and also breath. The breath, the source of "inspiration," is essential if you are to go beyond the body experience to experience your mind.

You are now engaging the limbic system of your brain, as well as the R-complex, in the running process. The limbic system is the seat of our emotions, and the breath is a good indicator of our emotions. It becomes agitated in anger, stopped in fear; it gasps in amazement, chokes in sadness, sighs with relief. Studies of the relationship between breath and emotion support the link between breath and the limbic system.

Breathing, which is both an involuntary and a voluntary bodily process, can to a large extent either be ignored or regulated. Students of yoga find they can learn to control their emotions surprisingly quickly by working with the breath. The holistic runner discovers that breath is a direct connection between his body and his mind, and also between nature and himself. As we breathe in oxygen and exhale carbon dioxide, we participate in the universal energy exchange along with other animals and plants.

Concentrate on using your diaphragm and belly, not your chest, to expand and contract your lungs. Your chest and upper rib cage are extremely inefficient instruments for good breathing. They require the expenditure of more effort and energy to accomplish the same amount of breathing, and they cannot produce breathing as deep as that from the diaphragm and abdominal muscles. If "belly breathing" gives you trouble, practice this simple exercise at home. Lie on the floor with a book on the upper part of your abdomen and concentrate on maximizing the movement of that book, up and down, as you breathe.

When you begin your run, try to breathe in as you take four steps and then to breathe out on the next four steps. If this seems too slow, switch to a 3-3 pattern. After the first mile or so, you may find that you are most comfortable with a 2-2 pattern: breathing out as you run two steps and in on the next two. Some runners discover that they operate most efficiently when they quickly and forcefully exhale, using only one stride, and then let the lungs refill on two strides, for a 2 count. If it helps, grunt or groan as you exhale.

In *Zen in the Art of Archery* the Zen master tells his student: ". . . concentrate entirely on your breathing, as if you had nothing else to do. Through this breathing, you will not only discover the source of all spiritual strength, but will also cause this source to flow more abundantly, and to pour more easily through your limbs."

When you come to a hill, accelerate your rate of breathing. You will be pleasantly surprised at how this seems to flatten out the incline. In so doing, you will be approximating a yogic exercise called *kapalabhati*, a strong, bellowslike pumping of the abdominal muscles that flushes the lungs with air.

Studies have been done on what is known as "alveolar air," the air in the deepest part of the respiratory system—in the lungs' air sacs, which are surrounded by the alveoli. It is in this area that the inspired air gives its oxygen to the body and takes on carbon dioxide for expiration. Alveolar air, the only active or utilized air in the act of respiration, is completely expired only at the end of a strong, deep expiration. Yogis, students of Zen, and athletes can maximize the efficiency of the breathing process by providing more and longer contact of alveolar air with alveoli air cells: Thus, the relationship between breath and *prana*, or energy. In efficient breathing, oxygen, the essential component of animal energy, is delivered in abundance, while carbon dioxide, the gas laden with impurities, is fully removed.

Step 3: The Mind

If you have been running regularly for three months or more and are now able to relax your body and control your breath as you run, you should try to increase your distance to six miles. Use the steady rhythms of your stride and your breath to alert your mind, to quiet it, to let it come into focus—to meditate. To meditate means to develop the capacity for observing your mind function without being over-whelmed with the usual barrage of thoughts leaping about up there like monkeys in a barrel. Medical doctors, like Dr. Mayo Emory, Sr., of the American Medical Joggers Association, recognize the link between running and meditation. "Running is like meditation," says Dr. Emory. "There are very few times when we are really *with* ourselves. You can run as a ritual, like a moment of prayer."

As you move beyond the fifth and sixth miles, quiet your mind and let it dissolve the protective "role layer," as the Gestalt therapists call it. Stop thinking of yourself as a husband or wife, professor or secretary, father or mother, lover or loser. Turn off your mental computer; you don't need it now. It won't help you run faster or farther—in fact, it is blocking you from improving your performance. Now it should be natural to turn down the noise volume of your mind and just focus on the images.

Focusing on the images does not mean forcing your mind down to a lower level of functioning. On the contrary, you are now engaging the highest evolutionary aspect of the brain, the neocortex. You are reducing the clutter of urgent but trivial matters from the neocortex, clearing it for higher thought.

Vedanta psychology and Jnana yoga offer a system for distinguishing among the various levels of thought. The "lower mind," or *manas*, collects sense impressions and coordinates them with motor responses. What happens at this level is comparable to the way a TV set might display sensory input and memory trace (known as *chitta*). The next higher level is "I-ness," or *ahankara*, at which sensory impressions are transformed into personal, unique experiences. For example, *manas* offer the objective datum, "The sunset is seen," and *ahankara* would transfer it into a participatory perception: "I see a sunset." The third level of mental functioning involves the judgment required after the perception has been individualized. This power of judgment is called the "crown jewel" of discrimination and understanding, or *buddhi*, which means enlightenment and gives its name to the religion founded by Prince Siddhartha.

Rather than subdividing the mind into *manas*, *ahankara*, and *buddhi*, the raja yoga of Patanjali offers a holistic theory in which the mind is compared to a lake. At rest it is calm and clear, but disruptive thoughts can stir it up and obscure its best nature. Such thoughts, called *vrittis*, are like waves in the lake, which may arise from the lake bed (memories) or from elsewhere (sense perceptions). The goal is to calm the lake so that the water is crystal clear, and one's inner consciousness can be perceived. Patanjali says that yoga is the process of calming the lake or concentrating the mind, and that only some people are prepared for such concentration. When *samadhi*, the deepest form of contemplation, is successfully achieved, the consciousness underlying the thoughts becomes apparent. Before achieving this, a person, in accord with conventional Western theory, identifies consciousness with thoughts and simply assumes that he *is* his thoughts. Descartes proudly declared, "I think, therefore I am." Patanjali and other yogis say, "What you *really* are is obscured by your thinking."

Therefore, when your thoughts begin to fade out as you simultaneously run and meditate, you are not descending to a lower level of brain function but rather shifting from the left to the right hemisphere of the neocortex. When sensory input is limited, memory traces and images are allowed to rise from *chitta*, the memory bank that, at its deepest, includes the unconscious. Fantasies and recollections are brought up in powerful display, as when one is under the influence of a hallucinogenic drug. A long, lonely run can afford the isolation and restricted sensory input required to communicate with one's inner world.

The Zen master, Suzuki, in his Introduction to *Zen in the Art of Archery*, makes it clear that right-hemisphere thinking is also a goal of Zen:

> Man is a thinking reed but his great works are done when hs is not calculating and thinking. "Childlikeness" has to be restored with long years of training in the art of self-forgetfulness. When this is attained, man thinks yet he does not think. He thinks like the showers coming down from the sky; he thinks like the waves rolling on the ocean; he thinks like the stars illuminating the nightly heavens; he thinks like the green foliage shooting forth in the relaxing spring breeze. Indeed, he is the showers, the ocean, the stars, the foliage.

Step 4: Buddhi, or Understanding

As you approach the eighth mile, familiar sights seem different. A line of cars on the highway becomes a flock of geese. Flowers emanate color and beauty that almost overpower. Your body is functioning in a more intimate relation to your mind. Sounds—especially the sound of your breathing—take on new and strange qualities.

We know that human perception is limited. Our vision covers only a small fraction of the known range of light; dogs can hear sound frequencies beyond our ears. The world is not, after all, what we sense it to be. Our senses or *manas* are pitifully inadequate. Our I-ness, or *ahankara,* also filters out much that is available to the senses but unwanted because of the need to avoid sensory overload or unwanted associations. These unwanted perceptions are what Western psychiatrists would call the unconscious.

What happens to you as a long-distance runner (or to the meditating yogi) is that your sense of I-ness, or consciousness, is expanding. Repressed material is brought into awareness. Just as you'll find you can run better, farther, and faster when you concentrate on relaxing your muscles, you will now find that the release of repressed material in your unconscious frees the energy previously used to hold it back. Researchers in yoga have found that an increasing amount of energy wells up in those who successfully, through meditation or other processes, enter the unknown world and explore their unconscious. In yoga, the process is symbolized by the rising serpent, *kundalini* (*kunda* means a bowl or basin). The *kundalini* is said to be coiled in the basin of the pelvis, swelling as it consumes energy from its host. As the process of expanding the I-ness develops, the *kundalini* rises, the energy it was consuming is released, and the host feels a welling of vitality.

Step 5: Bliss

Eight miles are behind you and you have given yourself to the run. All that required conscious control before—your stride, your posture, your breath—is now working without needing your overt attention. Your breath is slower and steadier; sweating has decreased, as has your heart rate. You feel at one with the landscape and the air and the horizon. You feel a steadily increasing sense of reverie, approaching euphoria, welling up within you.

The yoga scholar B. Ramamurthi wrote in "Neurological Explanations of Yogic Control of Visceral Functions" that the result of intense concentration over a sustained period puts "the mind in touch with a reality beyond time and space. When this is done successfully, the yoga rises above ordinary physiological requirements and capabilities." The extraordinary Lung-gom-pas runners of Tibet provide proof that running is a means of achieving this sustained concentration. Lung-gom is a form of yoga practiced in Tibet that combines mental concentration, breathing exercises, and incredible feats of running. The Lung-gom-pas runners run for several successive days and nights without stopping for any refreshment. As they run, oblivious to those they pass, chanting *ngags* (something like mantras) to themselves, they appear to be in deep meditation, and it is thought by their priests that they would die if interrupted, because the god instilled by the *ngags* would leave them.

According to Alexandra David-Neel in her book, *Magic and Mystery in Tibet,* Lung-gom-pas prepare for careers as runners not by running, but by practicing breathing exercises in seclusion and darkness for three and a half years. During this training period, they sit on thick cushions, inhale deeply, hold their breath, then jump up with their legs crossed and land in the same position, exhaling. They attribute their amazing endurance and speed to the control of what they call "internal air."

Similar feats of running endurance are also part of the ritual of the Tarahumara Indians of Mexico. As many as a hundred men will run 175 miles during a game that involves kicking a wooden ball. The ritual begins during midmorning and continues until early afternoon of the following day. Even when there is no contest, tribesmen will often run great distances, usually kicking the same kind of ball used in the games. Their means of achieving the intense concentration necessary for these superhuman feats is related somehow to the kickball itself, which acts much like a mantra to a yogi, or like breathing exercises to the Lung-gom-pas. Such remarkable running seems to be accomplished almost effortlessly. David-Neel reports that the Lung-gom-pas move with extreme grace, their stride has "the regularity of a pendulum and they seem endowed with the elasticity of a ball." They run as if unaware of the steepness of terrain or heat of the day.

It is not surprising that such extreme feats are achieved apparently without strain. Many subjects in biofeedback training discover that the harder they try to produce the desired effect, the less successful they will be. On the other hand, when they relax, they enhance their ability to control internal processes and even brain waves. This kind of control, which is linked to tranquil detachment and is often called "passive volition," seems to involve a shift to a state in which thinking or "willing" is organized nonverbally. Characteristic of this state is the use of images, the moving from the left to the right hemisphere of the neocortex. A common mistake made by those new to yoga—or to tennis or running, for that matter—is that they try too hard. They use active volition in an attempt to quiet their minds and compel relaxation, unlike the meditating yogi, who is given a mantra upon which he can focus his attention; the Lung-gom-pas runners who use a *ngag*; and the Tarahumara Indians, who concentrate on the ball. Running, too, offers organic repetitions. For example, the holistic runner can concentrate on his breathing or the rhythm of his feet striking the trail.

During common waking consciousness, the mind jumps from one thought to another, causing a rapid, jerky brain-wave pattern known as beta waves, on the electroencephalograph. A more tranquil mental state achieved through holistic running or meditation is characterized by alpha waves, and an even deeper level of consciousness, in which virtually all sensory impression is cut off from awareness, results in theta rhythms on the EEG. The theta pattern is the one associated with the state of reverie, which consists exclusively of images and no words, and is often impossible for the runner or yogi to describe any more specifically than "a state of euphoria."

Step 6: The Self

You have passed the ten mile mark. You sense that the things around you were not just created by God but continue to contain God, and that you are connected to them. You feel the center of energy in yourself; you are identified with the energy of which external nature is the image. You are not an island alone, but an embryo supported by all of nature around you. You have begun, as Emerson put it, to

"unlock your human doors and achieve a communion
with transcendant forces."

Buddhists describe the difficulty of letting go of our
limited consciousness in favor of a vastly expanded
one as comparable to the experience of a monkey
locked in a house with five windows, each represent-
ing one of the five senses. The monkey is secure, but
bored. All that exists for him are the bare walls and
the images outside the windows. He is in a cage and
the only reality is what he can sense. His unconscious
mind is no more than a synthesis of the sense perceptions he acquires in the little house. He lacks imagination or inspiration.

But if he gets out, escapes, he encounters an expanded state of consciousness and either experiences
oceanic joy and clarity or becomes psychotic. In fact,
those who return from such experiences often sound
crazy to us—we are so dominated by our left-hemi-
sphere culture. The Roman philosopher Plotinus
expressed the state of pure consciousness this way:

> You can only apprehend the infinite by a faculty
> superior to reason by entering into a state in which
> you are your finite self no longer . . . This is ec-
> stasy. It is the liberation of your mind from the
> finite consciousness . . . when you thus cease to be
> finite, you become one with the infinite.

Talk to runners after a long workout or a race. The
holistic runners will sound like E. M. Forster's Harold
as he literally rows his heart out against the tide in the
short story, "The Point of It":

> He made himself all will and muscle. He began not
> to know where he was. The thrill of the stretcher
> against his feet, and of the tide up his arms, merged

with his friend's voice towards one nameless sensation; he was approaching the mystic state that was the athlete's true though unacknowledged goal: he was beginning to be.

4

From Bliss to Blisters: Fitness Basics

As for that image, its head was of fine
gold, its breast and its arms of silver,
its belly and its thighs of brass, its
legs of iron, its feet part of iron and
part of clay. Thou sawest till that a
stone was cut out without hands, which
smote the image upon its feet that were
of iron and clay, and broke them in pieces.
From the *Book of Daniel 2:32–33*

Eight miles . . . ten miles—that's not bliss, you say,
that's agony! More likely, it's impossible! At this
point some fully accredited Eastern mystics would
shrug their shoulders unsympathetically, roll their
eyes up into their heads, and start meditating. Not
very helpful for the willing recruit who needs to learn
how to prepare for the physical stress of long-distance
running. How disappointing it would be to sense that a
higher stage of consciousness was just beyond the next
turning of your morning run, and then to have to
stop because of unbearable pain in your feet, or your
knees, or your back.

And so Chapters Four and Five of this book will attempt to offer help to those who would rather be running than reviewing all the available literature on
common physical ailments caused by running. In this
chapter, we will concentrate on the runner's anatomy

66

and how to keep it fit through simple exercises. Inevitably, though, problems occur that require simple first-aid treatment. By far, the most common problems encountered are caused by abuse of the feet. We will look at how to care for them and describe some of the shoes designed to preserve and protect them. Then the next chapter will focus on the care and feeding of the rest of the body—the cardiovascular system in particular.

Running Style

Running, like sex, is an activity that almost anybody can do, anyplace and anytime. As with sex, there is little or no equipment that must be purchased and then mastered for running; both activities come naturally; and, in both, a few basic elements of style can greatly improve your performance (and enjoyment). It is too bad that many people refuse to believe that their sex life can be improved by paying a little attention to performance. Similarly, many runners refuse to make any conscious attempt to alter their style, to the detriment of their performance and—sometimes—at the risk of hurting themselves.

Pay a little attention to your running style and stride. The key to holistic running is to run as easily and efficiently as possible, which is also the only way to avoid common aches and pains that could keep you out of action. You don't have to look pretty; nor do you have to look like a world-class runner. Even world-class runners don't always look like world-class runners, as you will realize if you watch the early finishers in a long-distance race. Some are pigeon-toed, others bow-legged. Some carry their arms high like

Sylvester Stallone in *Rocky*, others keep them so low as to be barely visible. The following suggestions may help you feel better and run more easily. If they do, use them. If they don't, experiment with variations of your own until you find your most relaxed and efficient running style.

Running "Tall"

Former track coach Bill Bowerman of the United States Olympic team and the University of Oregon studied slow-motion films of runners and determined that the best posture for a long-distance runner is when "the trunk is carried in an upright position and the feet track directly under the body." So, as already mentioned in Chapter One, do not lean forward. Try to keep your head relaxed but erect. It helps to focus on a point off in the distance directly in front of you. Also, as mentioned before, you can pretend that the top of your head is attached to a skyhook directly above, which will force your body, neck, and head to stay erect. You will be pleasantly surprised at how much easier your breathing will be if you maintain this posture, and how much farther your leg muscles can carry you.

If you imagine a plumb line dropped from your ear, it should fall straight through the shoulder line, then the hip, and down to the ground. To help keep things in line, try tilting the front part of your pelvis up and tucking your buttocks under, but don't lean backward.

If trying to follow all of these instructions makes you tense, relax and forget about them. Try them again each time you begin to run, but don't let them throw you into a state of tense confusion. In time, the conscious effort needed to maintain your new posture will disappear and your efficiency will have vastly improved.

Foot Strike

As your feet strike the ground approximately 1,600 times per mile while you run, they perform two important functions. First, they act as mobile adapters—somewhat like shock absorbers—and, second, they serve as rigid levers on push-off. If your gait is normal, the heel of your running shoe will be worn at the rear, slightly to the outside, and at the ball of the foot as well. This is because most long-distance runners will make contact first with the outside edge of the heel for maximum shock-absorption, then their feet will roll so that the forefoot comes down flat. As the leg comes over the foot, the heel tilts inward, transforming the foot into a rigid lever for maximum propulsion. Most sprinters strike first on the outside of the foot, but way up on the balls of the feet. As the runners' distance increases, the contact point moves further back toward the heel. However, Chris Stewart recently finished third in the New York marathon by running on the balls of his feet all the way. Usually, long-distance runners will tire faster and suffer greater risk of injury by running this way, but if you find that it works for you and you can handle it, let it be. Hal Higdon, a champion runner and an editor of *Runner's World*, claims that most long distance runners only *think* they are landing on their heels, while they really run sort of flat-footed.

Stride

The classic runner, as we imagine him, floats cross

country in slow motion, stretching one beautiful leg in front of the other, covering perhaps half a mile with each stride. In fact, long-distance runners should work within a relatively short stride, keeping their feet under them, not "striding out." Joe Henderson, another editor of *Runner's World*, says that "the ideal stride is free of high kick-up in the back, or high knee lift. The runner's feet should land directly behind his knees." One of the beginning jogger's biggest problems is overstride, which can result in painful and debilitating shinsplints or Achilles tendinitis, due to the exaggerated stress absorbed on heel strike after a stride that was too long or too high.

I cannot overemphasize the importance of maintaining a modest stride. When I started to increase my mileage and improve my speed for racing, I contracted extremely stiff, sore hips. Fearing that arthritis or worse had set in, or that I had one leg longer than the other, I went to my podiatrist, who found nothing functionally wrong with me. He then asked about my stride and recommended a shorter one. I tried it and the hip pain diminished significantly. Besides being healthier, a modest stride makes it possible for me to cover more miles at a faster pace. Swing forward with the big quadricep muscles of your thighs, but also feel motion in your ankle joints. The more motion you can produce in your ankles, the better runner you will be.

Arms and Hands

The arms, remember, used to be legs. Think of them as forelegs, used for drive and balance, just as they were in the olden days. In a short-stride running style, the arms move opposite the legs. In other words, as the right arm goes forward, the left leg goes forward. This style reduces the lateral rotation of the spine, minimizing strain on the back.

Don't forget your hands. Some beginners think that "cool" runners keep their hands open and limp. Not so. Hold your hands in loose fists. Your thumbs should be on your index fingers, palms slightly upturned, wrists firm without being tense, your hands in line with your arms and your elbows relaxed. Don't roll your shoulders or let them sway and dip; keep them as level as you can. Maintain a nice, easy driving motion in your elbows and forearms. Think of your arms as pendulums, moving from the area of your pants pockets up and across to your diaphragm, but don't let the hands cross over a center line drawn down the middle of your body. Remember that a good runner has strong arms. Exercising for this purpose, like doing push-ups, will help.

Nerves

We have seen that the secret of holistic running is to be found in relaxation. Especially after trying to adjust your running style, you are likely to be tense. Joe Henderson points to three places to check for tension as you run:

The large muscles at the base of the neck, in back.
The jaw muscles just below and in front of the ears.
The muscles around the eyes and the ones that wrinkle the forehead.

When you sense tightness or strain in these places, concentrate on loosening them up; this will cause you to relax all over. I am constantly amazed at how well this technique works, especially on steep hills, after long mileage, or in other stressful situations.

Symptoms of Trouble

Observers of the miraculous Lung-gom-pas and Tarahumara runners have noted that both have a running style that seems weightless and a smooth, easy stride. Try to emulate them. If your feet slap the road with each step, you are not running *with* your feet but *on* them, with insufficient lift. If you appear to be bouncing instead of gliding, you are probably over-striding. Your head should stay almost parallel with the ground. Look in a storefront window. Are you leaning forward? Remember that skyhook. Are your arms and hands flapping? If so, they aren't acting as evolved forelegs, providing necessary power and balance. Finally, check your tension points. Relax.

Running Surfaces

Runners are to be seen everywhere these days—barefoot on beaches; along railroad tracks; cross country through fields and woods; on mountain trails, golf courses, highways, paved and unpaved roads; and, of course, on running tracks of all kinds. There is no consensus as to the best running surface. "Best" depends on your personal goals.

When I started running, I was most happy on grass, or a track surfaced in Tartan or other soft artificial material. The problem with tracks is that they are boring—hardly the ideal environment for holistic running. Grass, on the other hand, is lovely and soft but deceptively uneven and treacherous. I have often twisted my ankle gliding across lovely turf, miles from anywhere. After one such incident, I was driven home in a squad car by a kindly policeman who had happened on my sweaty, shivering body. Now I prefer asphalt bike paths and other *flat* paved surfaces. I emphasize the importance of flat surfaces because the typical road is cambered toward the side. If you run against traffic (as you should), you will always have your left foot on a lower level than your right—an unhealthy arrangement. Beaches involve a similar pitch problem, but you can at least even out the stress by turning around halfway through your run.

George Sheehan prefers grass and other soft surfaces because they are easier on the shins. Sawdust trails like the one in Eugene, Oregon, send many runners into ecstasy. All soft surfaces are somewhat forgiving of imperfections in your own style and physiological structure. On hard surfaces, symptoms of structural problems are more likely to develop. You are more likely to grab with your toes on hard surfaces, which puts stress on the shin muscles. Nevertheless, better runners such as Frank Shorter have renounced grass for paved paths and roads. Shorter finds that he cannot concentrate on his running if he has to worry about gopher holes. But paved roads don't mean that you can't have an accident. During the 1977 Women's National AAU Marathon Championship in the Twin Cities of Minnesota, Joan Ullyot tripped in a pothole. She fell, scraping both knees, and, as a result, lost a chance to win. Everybody agrees that bridle paths, with their hidden holes that can cause falls and strained ligaments, are even more treacherous. A reasonably hard dirt path or road or a paved walk with a two-inch surface of fresh powdery snow are about as close as you can come to the ideal surface. But don't let the terrain deter you. As you'll see shortly, the quality of running shoes available today makes the choice of running surface much less critical than ever before.

Exercises

Running strengthens some muscles and weakens others. The muscles that are strengthened mainly involve the gravity muscles, like those in the back of your leg that help you leave the surface and fly through the air. Your antigravity muscles, like those in the front of your legs, help you fight gravity as you hit the surface, thereby minimizing the jarring of the body as it returns to earth. The muscles in the front of your thighs also help decelerate the body and keep it from falling over the leg. So the rear muscles from the foot through the back tend to become strong and tight in runners, whereas the front muscles become too weak. Hamstrings and heel cords, in particular, may become very tight. Some runners, when their calf (back) muscles overpower their (front) shin muscles, suffer from shinsplints, and others even have symptoms of swayback because running tightens the lower back muscles, while it does nothing much for the stomach muscles. So it is easy to see that aches, pains, and injuries are almost inevitable, unless runners spend half their time running backward or perform exercises designed to stretch the gravity muscles and strengthen the antigravity muscles, thus rebalancing the body.

Trainers and doctors have established a proper ratio—approximately 60–40—for each group of gravity muscles in relation to antigravity muscles. The calf should be twice as strong as the shin. Shinsplints can hardly be corrected in runners who have calf muscles four to eight times more powerful than their shin muscles. But such a problem doesn't have to arise if you develop a program of regular exercise.

The following set of simple exercises (including some yoga asanas) have been culled from the hundreds urged upon me. Each one was recommended by a medical doctor or podiatrist, and is easy and painless enough not only for me to advise you to do but for me to do myself. If you do one or two at a time, throughout the day, at odd moments, they won't seem boring.

Stretching the Gravity (Back) Muscles

Toe touching. Stand with knees locked (or nearly so), touch your toes, and hold for a count of ten. Relax a few seconds and repeat until your calf muscles get tired. Don't bounce—you might tear the muscles you only want to stretch. After a while, when you try pushing your hands under the balls of your feet, you will be doing the *pada hastana* yoga asana.

Wall push-ups. Stand more than an arm's length away from a wall. Lean into the wall, finally catching it with your hands. If your heels have left the ground, slowly lower them again, keeping your knees locked. Hold for a count of ten and repeat until your calves and hamstrings begin to feel tired.

Pretzel bow. With arms at sides and right knee locked, cross your left leg over and slightly behind your right, placing your left toes on the ground while your right foot remains flat. Put your right hand on your left shoulder. Bend from the waist, bringing your head as close as possible to your knees. Hold for the count of ten. Bounce up and down a bit to enhance the stretch effect. Reverse and repeat until your hamstrings feel tired.

Stair stretch. Stand with your toes on a stairstep or a telephone book, heels over the edge. Lower the heels below the toes and hold for a count of ten. Release, rest a few seconds, and repeat until your calf muscles are tired.

The plow (halasana) *or leg-over*. Lie on your back for this asana. Raise your legs straight up, supporting your shoulders with your arms. Gradually bring your legs down until they touch the floor behind your head. Keep your legs straight. At first this will seem impossible, but stay with it. When you begin, don't stay down more than a few seconds. When you become used to it, you will be able to stay down for several minutes. I usually start with two ten-second dips to the floor, then sustain the third for three or four minutes.

Strengthening the Antigravity (Front) Muscles

Sit-ups. Lie on your back with knees raised somewhat. Bring your trunk off the floor to a halfway position. You can fancy this up by wrapping a weight in a towel and holding it behind your neck. I do sixty of these, to strengthen abdominal muscles.

Leg-ups. Using two- or three-pound ankle weights, lie on your back and slowly raise your legs from the hips to a perpendicular position. Keep them straight. Then slowly lower them, not quite to the floor. I do twenty of these.

Leg lifts. With the ankle weights still on, sit on a bench. Gradually lift your legs until they are straight out, with your thighs slightly off the bench. I do twenty of these.

Push-ups. With your arms, lift yourself from a prone position until your elbows lock. I do a bit extra by bringing myself up with enough momentum so I can clap hands before lowering my body gradually to the mat. I do twenty-four "flying" push-ups and twelve more conventional ones.

Another way of maintaining good physical conditioning is to vary your workouts. Run at different speeds and for varying distances to exercise more and different muscles. Occasional workouts on the track at a faster pace will improve your endurance as well. Don't let your workouts get so routine that they bore you. Finally always end up with a cool-down period of walking and easy stretching to help counteract stiffness and muscle cramping.

Common Overuse Injuries

The foot has twenty-six bones, four times that number of ligaments, and networks of tendons, veins, and arteries. The normal foot functions without placing any undue stress upon itself or on the structure it supports—that is, the ankle, leg, knee, thigh, hip, and spine. But the problem with this description of what the normal foot is supposed to do is that the normal foot is hardly the *average* foot, which is likely to have one or more abnormalities.

My feet supported me with no symptoms of protest for more than thirty years, until I started long-distance running—and then, at about twenty miles a week, my abnormalities caught up with me. The same thing will probably happen to holistic runners running thirty miles a week and more. For the fact is that most of us run with some biomechanical abnormality. Long-distance running was no doubt natural to our barefoot ancestors (it is natural to the Lung-gom-pas), but it is, alas, unnatural to most of us. However, a foot that is properly cared for does not have to suffer. So let us examine the common problems caused by overuse through running and see what measures can be taken for prevention or cure.

A long-distance runner who runs thirty-three miles per week plants *each* foot about one million times per year. With each step, the foot must adapt to provide the body with support, locomotion, and balance, and to compensate for changes in body position, weight distribution, and the inclination of the course. It is not surprising, then, that barring the unattainable perfect foot in a perfect shoe, running perfectly, on a perfect surface, overstress will almost inevitably lead to overuse injuries, such as shinsplints, Achilles tendinitis, heel spurs, bursitis, chondromalacia of the knee, various muscle tendon strains, stress fractures, periostitis and fasciitis.

Four times in six years *Runner's World* surveyed approximately one thousand readers about their aches and pains. According to the results, 60 to 70 percent of runners claimed to have been injured during running in the previous twelve months, and many were hurt more than once. Overuse injuries were far and away the most common occurring with the following frequency:

Injured area	Percent of runners
Knee	25
Achilles' tendon	18
Shin	15
Ankle	11
Heel	10
Arch	8
Calf	7
Hip	7

My example is a typical one. Like most beginners, I started running short distances in tennis shoes; an uninformed acquaintance soon suggested switching to the lightest, cheapest canvas track shoes. Gradually I began to feel pain in my heels. As my mileage increased, so did the pain, and, occasionally it became as acute as the pain caused by a dentist's drill. I began a mad search for relief. I bought better shoes, walked and ran on the balls of my feet. Nothing helped. Finally, I had to face the bitter fact that I couldn't run anymore. It was a classic case of overuse syndrome.

Then I had to deal with the typical medical buffoonery in the face of overuse syndrome. I visited a high-priced orthopedist, who took X-rays, which indicated virtually nothing. He recommended a cortisone injection. I understood that cortisone would relieve the symptoms—temporarily. This is useful to the athlete who must run the next day's race or play the Super Bowl, but, I asked, how would a cortisone injection make it possible for me to resume regular running, when whatever had caused the pain before would undoubtedly cause it again. The orthopedist harrumphed, dropped the cortisone-injection idea, and suggested that the X-rays indicated possible swelling.

He then recommended a course of aspirin, and heel soaks twice daily in hot water. When I explained that I was allergic to aspirin, he proposed Tylenol as an alternative. So, for weeks, I took about a dozen Tylenols a day and soaked my feet in wastebaskets of hot water, morning and night. Later I learned that Tylenol, unlike aspirin, has no effect on inflammation. At the time this man, who was of no practical use to me, had his picture in all the papers for having invented an artificial joint. The problem was, I began to think, he did not feel intellectually challenged by my feet.

When I asked my internist what to do next, he first suggested that I give up running. Finally, convinced that I was loath to do so, he surreptitiously referred me to a podiatrist, Dr. George R. Gabriel. Medical doctors ordinarily refuse to acknowledge that the least human suffering, even a hangnail, can be relieved by anyone who does not have an M. D. certificate. Although podiatrists, who used to be called chiropodists, are licensed doctors, they are not medical doctors. They are authorized to perform procedures ranging from relief of corns and calluses to complex surgery on the feet. Dr. Gabriel's X-rays (or, more likely, his more specialized interest and insight into problems of the feet) revealed what he later came to call, "painful calcaneal spurs on right and left feet with periostitis and plantar fasciitis." But these ugly-sounding maladies were merely the symptoms of overuse, not the cause, and could easily be treated with a little hydrotherapy, ultrasound, and taping. The way to get me running again was to treat my fairly common abnormalities, forefoot varus and tibial varum.

Forefoot Varus

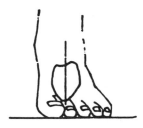

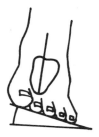

Normal Foot Plant. A line drawn through heel bone would be perpendicular to ground.

Forefoot Varus. Forefoot has outward tilt, resulting in roll of foot as it compensates.

Tibial Varum

Tibial Varum. Lower leg is bowed out of line. Landing on the outside of the foot, with a twisting motion needed to meet the ground.

With this kind of abnormality, when the heel is perpendicular to the ground and the leg is lined up straight above it, the inner side of the forefoot does not touch the floor. In my case, the incline gap between me and the floor begins at the raised inner side of the forefoot, slanting progressively lower to the outer side of the foot which is the only part to touch the floor. In order to bring the metatarsals (the bone structure that include the toes) to the ground, the whole apparatus—foot, ankle, leg, knee, thigh, hip, and back—must rotate inward. Such abnormal stressful twisting and turning contributes to all types of foot, leg, and back problems. You can experience it for yourself in an easy demonstration if you stand up and, with the right foot bearing your body weight, lower your right inner arch as much as you can. Notice how this forces your entire leg structure to rotate inward—your kneecap turns in, your entire body slumps. It is a little bit like what happens to a table with one short leg when weight is placed on it in the vicinity of the short leg.

My problem was compounded by tibial varum, a bowing outward of the lower leg bones. Obviously, this exaggerates the problem of not being able to stand normally, since even more pronation is required to bring the foot into full contact with the floor.

These kinds of problems begin with the fetus, whose entire limb system is twisted inward. In normal growth, fetal limbs unfold from the varus position and, in a child age six, should have unfolded completely. When, as in my case, they do not, problems like forefoot varus and tibial varum are the result. If too much unfolding takes place in the fetus and during early infancy, the opposite problems will occur, typically in the form of "subtalar valgus," which means that the upper leg must supinate excessively in compensation. (Supination is the opposite of pronation.) You can demonstrate the supination effect by rolling your right arch as high as possible. Observe how the opposite kinds of twistings and turnings are then required from the foot all the way to the lower back.

In running, the normal foot pronates and supinates. It pronates to become a shock absorber and mobile adapter at heel strike, and, in order to become a rigid lever for propulsion, it supinates. My feet had an impossible job pronating excessively to compensate for the forefoot varus and tibial varum; and so they were not able to supinate properly when required. As commonly happens when abnormal feet are called upon to run long distances, mine broke down.

One of the important things to remember about overuse syndrome is that the same biomechanical abnormalities may provide different symptoms in different people. Forefoot varus, for example, can produce pain and problems anywhere from the lower back and hip to the foot. In my case, it caused stress on the

Plantar Fasciitis. The bands along the bottom of the foot are the "plantar fascia." The "heel spur" is the point at the base of the heel bone.

plantar fascia, which are strong fibrous bands under the foot with attachments to the underside of the heel, the area in which I experienced the pain. The constant strain there caused the fascia themselves to become inflamed, and bursitis to develop where they are attached to the heel bones; it also caused heel spurs. Dr. Gabriel describes this excessive pull that strains the fascial attachments as a "windlass effect."

The extraordinary thing about modern podiatry is that many problems are commonly solved while the runner keeps running. In my case, the solution involved building an orthotic support, a gizmo designed to provide structural realignment between the bottom of the foot and the floor, and to regulate the foot's twistings and turnings. As soon as treatment started, the heel pain began diminishing—and was completely gone within a few months. Throughout this period and since then, I have been increasing my mileage and improving my speed.

As the *Runner's World* survey indicated, a popular area for runners to experience pain is the heel. The reason is obvious. The heel carries 75 percent of your body weight when you merely stand, 120 percent while you walk, 200 percent while you run, 300 percent while you jog, and 400 percent when you jump.

Morton's Foot

Some podiatrists think that 80 percent of us have what is known either as Morton's Foot or Morton's Syndrome, a condition in which the second metatarsal is longer than the first. The first metatarsal head—the bone structure out of which the big toe emanates—becomes lax, loose, and floppy, or "hypermobile," which causes problems along the entire inner border of the foot. When necessary, a podiatrist can treat this defect by building up the area under the first metatarsal head at the base of the big toe.

Discrepancies in Leg Length

You may have one leg that is anatomically a little shorter than the other. Or, you may turn and twist your leg so that, in order to compensate for a problem like forefoot varus or valgus, one leg is *functionally* shorter than the other. If you are right-handed, your left leg will tend to be the short one, and vice versa. Only if you run long distances should you worry about whether or not you have this problem. It is with overuse due to running that you may get back, hip, or knee pain because you must tilt your pelvis and compensate for the discrepancy by twisting your spinal column. If yours is a functional rather than an anatomical problem, you may also experience muscle spasms along the shorter leg.

Compensating for the discrepancy will easily correct the problem, but first it must be diagnosed. X-rays won't catch it. What will reveal it—if the problem is structural and in the lower leg—is a carpenter's level placed across the knees while you are seated and your feet flat on the floor. If the level is three sixteenths of an inch or more off center, you have a significant imbalance. For another method that will detect an imbalance anywhere up to the hip, Dr. Lowell Scott Weil, director of the Illinois College of Podiatric Medicine, recommends that you stand in front of a mirror in your undershorts, making certain that they touch the top of the hipbone on each side. If the shorts appear crooked, you will know there is an imbalance. Dr. Steve Subotnick, the "running foot doctor," suffered great pain and acute frustration due to a knee problem and tried everything before discovering that he had one leg shorter than the other.

Genu Varum and Genu Valgum (Bowlegs and Knock-knees)

Genu varum, or bowlegs, are the knees' equivalent

of forefoot varus and tibial varum. This condition also causes the feet to strike the ground on the outside and thus pronate beyond the normal 4 degrees to compensate. Poor Subotnick, who is also bowlegged, says that he has to swing his feet way out or he'll kick himself. (Also, he gets a little push-off for propulsion as a result.) With bowlegs, overuse symptoms may involve knee pain, heel bumps, and ankle sprains.

If bowlegs are like forefoot varus and tibial varum, knock-knees are, obviously, like forefoot valgas and tibial valgum. The knock-kneed runner will experience a prolonged pronation that prevents the feet from ever becoming rigid enough to produce the lever action required for propulsion. Both problems are correctible, more or less, with proper biomechanical control.

Achilles Tendinitis

Although we are now being unscientific in discussing symptoms instead of causes, a few symptoms, like Achilles tendinitis, are so common that they deserve such spotlighting. People with short Achilles tendons are destined to have problems—even when they do the recommended stretching exercises, they must be careful. Runners who do not strengthen the gravity (front) muscles in their legs will have grossly overdeveloped calves, which will prevent the running foot from flexing up and down approximately 10 degrees. The heel and ankle will become too tight and undue stress will be placed on the Achilles tendon. Some correction for short Achilles tendons is possible, but nothing takes the place of proper stretching exercises.

Shinsplints

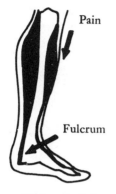

Pain

Fulcrum

Shinsplints. Strong posterior muscles work against weak anterior shin muscles.

This painful symptom usually results from a combination of structural and postural problems, compounded by overuse or overstriding. Weak feet, weak shin muscles, and short powerful gastrocnemius muscles set the stage for trouble, and hard surfaces and hard shoes aggravate matters. Hill running and speed work encourage grabbing with the toes, which also adds to the problem.

If you are prone to suffer from shinsplints, attend to these factors and experiment with changing them. For example, concentrate on floating your toes, instead of grabbing with them. Also try this special exercise for shinsplint sufferers which I've done with good results: Sit on a bench or table, slip your ankle weights down over your toes, and tighten the toes. Then bring your legs up slightly and flex your feet up and down. Tougher shins are the beneficial result.

Runner's Knee

Like forefoot varus, this common, painful problem is also caused by excessive pronation. Countertorsion between the lower leg and the thigh results in the knee taking the punishment in between. While the left leg is internally rotating because of excessive pronation, the opposite hip juts forward, externally rotating the left thigh. Most cases of runner's knee can be "cured" with orthopedic appliances designed to control the biomechanical imbalances that cause prolonged pronation of the foot.

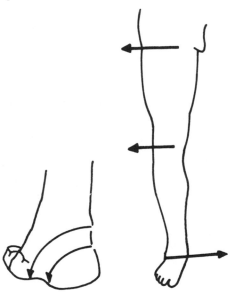

Pronated Foot. The first figure illustrates a pronated foot. The second figure illustrates the consequences of a pronated foot. The ankle is forced inward as the knee and hip are forced outward, causing pain anywhere from the foot to the lower back.

Blisters

Holistic runners will get blisters but some will get them more than others. You can minimize blisters by wearing good cotton-acrylic-blend socks with benign

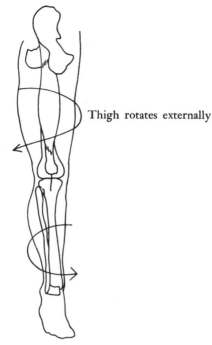

Thigh rotates externally

Leg rotates internally

Knee pain caused by "runner's knee." Trouble caused by counter-torsion between leg and thigh.

seams (but not tube socks) and good well-fitting shoes with quality insoles, such as those made by Spenco. Excessive sweating also causes blisters, so try powdering your feet if this is a problem of yours. Small blisters can be ignored, especially when you eliminate the cause, such as a wrinkled sock. Slightly larger blisters can be accommodated with a regular padded band-aid. If a blister is painful, try cutting a hole for it in a piece of moleskin bandage and then place the bandage on the area surrounding it, leaving the blister exposed but buffered. If it is too full to live with, wash the blister and skin around it thoroughly with soap and water. Then cut the covering skin near the blister's lower edge with a sterilized razor blade. After cutting, leave the covering skin alone as protection, but sterilize the area with nonalcoholic antiseptic and paint it with tincture of benzoin. Finally, cover it with a conventional padded band-aid.

Blisters are very dangerous. They can lead to blood poisoning and death. Calvin Coolidge's son died from complications from a blister.

Pain and Self-Help

Remember the *Runner's World* survey earlier in this chapter, which showed that 60 to 70 percent of runners will be injured each year (and the rate of injured runners goes up along with extra-mileage runs). The first thing a student of yoga learns is to listen to his body—to stretch it to the edge of pain, but not go over the edge. Similarly, holistic runners run through annoyances, but not through pain. Of course, if you experience chest pains or any other ominous symptoms suggesting problems more serious than overuse syndrome, you should seek professional help immediately. But, in many cases, the routine minor injuries you will suffer can be remedied at home.

A twisted ankle or foot can usually be treated with ice to help reduce inflammation. Avoid heat during the same period because it has the opposite effect.

You can self-diagnose some imbalance problems before running aggravates them. One way is to kneel, barefooted, on a chair and relax. If your heels line up with your feet and the balls of your feet are parallel with your heels, you probably have close-to-normal balance. If not, you should be concerned. With bare feet and legs, stand opposite a mirror to check for imbalance in your shin area. If the shins curve in like parentheses (), you have imbalance there (tibial varum). To confirm the diagnosis, look at your shoes. They should exhibit most wear on the outside edge of the heel and the ball of the foot. I realized that my intense heel pain had some relationship to running when I saw that my running shoes were exclusively wearing down on the outside edges.

You may want to try correcting imbalance problems yourself. If you have shinsplints, Dr. Sheehan suggests in addition to the prescribed exercises, adding a one-quarter- to one-half-inch felt heel lift to your shoes. Dr. Subotnick suggests building up your weak areas with felt and trainer's tape. Use elastic tape with the sticky side out, so it can be slipped on and off. If you have problems of imbalance and can't deal with home-tailored pads, Dr. Sheehan suggests trying commercial inserts such as Dr. Scholl's Athletic A or 610, and I agree. Drs. Gabriel and Subotnick, on the other hand, advise *against* "store-bought" inserts. Some doctors recommend taping with moleskin to cure Achilles tendinitis. If you want to try it, tape around the foot, keeping the first metatarsal head raised and the arch up. For heel pain, try taping the heel, first pushing some of the fatty tissue of the heel under the painful area, so you can run on the fat instead of on the heel spur or on the inflamed nerves.

Professional Care for Overuse Problems

Many common problems can be corrected at home, but if you encounter any you cannot take care of yourself, see a podiatrist trained in sports medicine. This is not always as easy as it sounds, for there is a scarcity of trained and interested podiatrists. Furthermore, the July 1977 issue of the *Journal of the American Podiatry Association* states that no more than five million people are presently being treated by podiatrists. If ten million Americans are now running, and 80 percent of them have foot and leg problems, that means that podiatrists are not seeing as many *total* patients as there are runners who may need help. However, the runner may take heart; the field is expanding dramatically. Compared to five years ago, twice as many doctors are now graduating from podiatry schools.

The problem is that podiatric treatment for runners usually involves many visits with long periods of doctor-patient contact for measurements and therapy. Biomechanical appliances, such as orthotic supports, are expensive to design, cast, construct, and adjust. And because runners tend to be inquisitive and hypochondriacal, some podiatrists would prefer to stay away from them. All this means that good podiatric treatment, *if* you can find it at all, will probably cost you money. So you will have to decide how much it is worth to you and how much you can afford. I find that even with the cost of treatment and appliances figured in, running remains a relatively inexpensive sport.

As you would expect in a growing and dynamic field, there are conflicting theories about the various ways to correct biomechanical defects. Drugs can alleviate only symptoms, not the causes. My own experience indicates that orthotic appliances will greatly reduce the risk of continuous knee, ankle, hip, and back pain due to biomechanical problems. Generally, they are custom-made of strong, light plastic, from plaster casts of your feet, but some podiatrists may substitute a more flexible appliance, as my podiatrist originally prescribed for me. However, the latter provide less precise functional control of the foot and is therefore not as likely to correct serious imbalances. Orthotic supports should strengthen the foot by providing a more stable structure on which the bones, muscles, and tendons can function. They control heel contact, midstance, and toe-off and have been proven effective in reducing overuse symptoms.

The rigid functional-control orthotic appliances are well tolerated by most but not all patients. Dr. Subotnick reports a 15 percent failure rate, caused mainly, he says, by misuse. Be careful, therefore, to ensure that your foot molds are well cast, and be patient while the appliances are adjusted after you begin using them. Pain on the outside of the knee, for example, may mean that the appliance must be ground down slightly in the medial heel area. Appliances can have slight wedges or posts added as well. Dr. Gabriel typically begins with an orthotic appliance that does not attempt to correct the runner's entire imbalance; he gradually adds control as the condition improves. With the help of sports podiatry, the architecture of your feet and legs, which God may have somewhat miscalculated, can be greatly improved. Biomechanics can't make a McDonald's hamburger stand into Monticello, so to speak, but it can usually keep a weak structure from getting weaker and collapsing.

Shoes

Morrie Mages, a Chicago sporting-goods magnate, believes that the volume of athletic shoes now being sold exceeds that of conventional shoes. As early as 1975, U.S. retail sales of athletic shoes amounted to more than $1.25 billion, almost double the total of seven years before, while sales of ordinary shoes remained almost constant in the same period. This flood of sports footwear sales is in part due to the new chic: Many people wear cheap running shoes, which the manufacturers call "leisure" shoes, all the time; choreographer Twyla Tharp has dedicated a new dance to Adidas; the *Wall Street Journal* carried a front-page piece on the explosion in the industry. And, besides, according to *Runner's World*, 24 million Americans are now having a go at jogging or running.

With so much trade out there, you would expect the manufacturers of *real* running shoes to be falling all over themselves to gain a competitive edge—and you would be correct. Bob Anderson, publisher of *Runner's World*, says, "The state of the art of running shoes has reached the point, in fact, that I can honestly say that there is not a single training flat in the top 25 as rated by *Runner's World* that isn't a good investment."

But, according to Dr. George Gabriel:

> It is impossible to design an "ideal" static housing of the foot which is a mobile, dynamic organ of locomotion and adaptation. The problem is made more complicated by variations in foot types, and physiological changes in a single foot during the course of a long-distance run. Finally, most of us do not have structurally sound feet capable of coping with both foot housing (the shoe) and environment. Therefore, any shoe gear must be considered a necessary evil to protect the foot from the potentially harmful effects of the elements.

However the shoe is designed, the runner's foot will break it in. "A shoe must house, protect and allow the foot to function," says Dr. Gabriel, but at the same time it must not inhibit these functions." In a short time, the runner's foot will cause the shoe to shape and bend to the structural and functional idiosyncracies of the foot. I recommend that runners—and walkers too, for that matter—look for the 'least insulting' shoe." In effect, Dr. Gabriel defies "anyone to place his foot side by side with his shoes and find a compatible relationship."

So, in spite of all the athletic-shoe ballyhoo, we can only expect our running shoes to make the best of a bad job. The following checklist of shoe characteristics, therefore, is designed to help you know what to look for if you want to begin your own search for the "least imperfect" training flat.

Heel. Men: width about 75 mm. Wider heel would tend to increase width of gait to avoid striking inner ankles. Women: typically, look for a somewhat narrower shoe. Should be inclined outward one cm to vertical axis of tibia. Reinforced with denser, stronger soling at posterior, outside heel edge.

Heel depth (insole to top of inside counter). Men: minimum 60–65 mm except for very low arched feet. Women: minimum 58–60 mm except for very low arched feet.

Achillies pad. Desirable, but check for careful placement of seams.

Heel counters. Look for padding with self-adjusting material for conforming to variations in heel shapes and widths. Should also reduce slippage. If possible, find a shoe with a slotted self-closure feature to allow this adjustment to be made.

Insole. Should be impact-cushioned at least ¼″ at toe and heel, removable and self-adhering to allow for adjustments, increasing of depth for orthotics, or depth adjustments for short leg balance, unusually high contractions of toes, insteps, arch, and other problems.

Insole material. Look for features that reduce frictional irritations due to shear forces, back-and-forth motions, and impact stress—and that allow for modification.

Waist area. Shoe should be reinforced and combined with proper lacing. The lacing adds support by a corseting action (cinching).

Lacing pattern. Blucher type, starting just behind metatarsal heads, to permit better sole breaking and flexibility of the propulsive area.

Tongue. Slotted to keep laces from shifting. Enveloped, self-closure with conforming filler for adapting to foot, reduce irritations and assisting in proper cinching of waist area.

Toe box. There should be at least 25 mm depth to decrease possible digital and nail pressure.

Sole. Look for good wearability and flexibility for toe-off and take-off motion, good cushioning, traction, and release of traction. Too much traction will increase effort and lead to fatigue. Deep cleating will hold dirt, stones, and extraneous matter, thereby losing traction and lessening flexibility, and, of course, adding weight. The sole should be laterally in line with the proper placement of the heel by avoiding in-flaring and allowing the lateral foot segments to rest fully on the insole and sole region.

Linings. Cushioning without rucking is desirable. Seams should be covered and placed to avoid obvious irritation.

Upper materials. Light, flexible, porous for warm weather. Impervious and flexible for cold and wet conditions.

Sizes. Wide range of widths could be important, such as *New Balance*, AA to EEEE, 3½ to 15. *Nike* to E width, 3 to 13. (See size ranges of each brand listed below.)

Bad running shoes, like bad walking shoes, will produce tired, sore, blistered feet. Ankle pain is another frequent problem linked to bad shoes. If the heel is too narrow, the ankle will have unstable support. If the shoe is too soft, the ankle will be constantly forced to turn to the outside. Shoes that are too tight may also cause ingrown toenails or ingrown hairs, which may in turn produce secondary skin infections and pinch calluses. Remember, don't look only at the thickness of the shoe's sole; the cushion effect depends on the *quality* of the material, *not* its thickness.

Watch out for "new developments" in running shoes. For example the new sexy, black Adidas Formula I has a specially extended flare in the rear of the heel area that may cause premature heel strike. Similarly, the widely flared Nike LD-1000 may cause knee pain because the wider flare at the side of the heel will make the foot slam down too hard and fast after heel strike, thus accelerating pronation and causing instability. The refined version, on the other hand—the Nike LD-1000-V—reduces the flare and, presumably, the problem; Dr. Subotnick says that it is especially good for people who twist their ankles easily. Dr. Gabriel warns against the new cleated soles, designed to improve traction. Too much traction might increase the motion of the foot in the shoe, he says, thus jamming the toes against the toe box and causing assorted aches and pains, including plantar fasciitis.

Recently *Runner's World* convened a panel of "experts"—runners, doctors, podiatrists, and coaches—to evaluate all the running shoes on the market. At the same time, they also subjected the shoes to tests at Penn State University Biomechanics Laboratory.

When the survey was released, in October, 1977, I obtained as many of the top shoes as I could find and have run extensively in them. So here are their specifications and rankings, as reported in *Runner's World*, followed by my own evaluations.

Adidas Runner

Introduced in 1975. Suggested price $37.95. Available in sizes 3½–15 (one width). Single size-nine weighs 318 gm.

Upper. Nylon mesh and leather trim in yellow and blue respectively. U-box ghillie lacing. Padded ankle collar.

Inside. Expanded rubber arch support. PVC foam textile insole. Heel depth 81 mm. Ankle depth 55/43 mm. Toe box 25 mm.

Sole. Waffle-profile tread. Three layers under forefoot, 16 mm thick. Three layers under heel, 27 mm thick. Heel lift 11 mm. Heel width 81 mm.

I like the nylon mesh upper for warm weather, but those of us who also run in the cold of winter need insulation, not ventilation. The new ghillie lacing is a real convenience. The shoe yields a "hard" feel, but is one of the most comfortable and durable I have ever used.

Dr. Lowell Weil evaluated some shoes with respect to their probable effect on runners' common ailments. This one, he believes, is good for people with runner's knee.

Brooks Villanova

Introduced in 1976. Suggested price $19.95. Available in sizes 4–12 and 13 (narrow, medium, wide). Single size-nine weighs 319.9 gm.

Upper. Nylon with nylon tricot and suede trim, blue and orange. U-throat lacing. Padded ankle and heel collar.

Inside. Foam rubber arch support. 2½ Iron Texon insole. Heel depth 76 mm. Ankle depth 48/44 mm. Toe box 32 mm.

Sole. Suction-cup threads. Two layers under forefoot, 12 mm thick. Three layers under heel, 25 mm thick. Heel lift 13 mm. Heel width 80 mm.

A terrific bargain in a durable, comfortable shoe. I have run hundreds of miles in this shoe, which is occasionally offered by the National Jogging Association at a price that is an even greater bargain.

Etonic KM

Introduced in 1976. Suggested price $25.95. Available in sizes M6-12 and 13, W8-11 (narrow, medium, wide.) Single size-nine weighs 324.8 gm.

Upper. Nylon with leather trim, blue and white. U-throat lacing. Padded ankle and heel collar.

Inside. Built-in arch support. Polyurethane/polyethylene insole. Heel depth 74 mm. Ankle depth 49/45 mm. Toe box depth 38 mm.

Sole. Star-design tread. Two layers under forefoot, 12 mm thick. Three layers under heel, 24 mm thick. Heel lift 12 mm. Heel width 80 mm.

This shoe is much like the Brooks Villanova with a one-piece arch and heel support added, which was designed by podiatrist Dr. Rob Roy McGregor. I always pull the foam rubber arch supports out of my running shoes to make room for the orthotic appliances. In this shoe, it wasn't necessary, although I don't get much advantage from the support because it goes under my orthotic appliances. These shoes travel with me a great deal; they seem quite versatile and are comfortable on different surfaces. It's a good shoe, according to Dr. Weil, if you are bothered by runner's knee or plantar fasciitis.

New Balance 320

Introduced in 1976. Suggested price $27.95. Available in sizes 3½–15 (widths AA to EEE). Single size-nine weighs 293 gm.

Upper. Polyester mesh with sueded split-leather, blue and white. Blucher lacing. Padded ankle and heel collar.

Inside. Polyurethane arch support. Polyurethane insole. Heel depth 70 mm. Ankle depth 48/46 mm. Toe box depth 21 mm.

Sole. Brush sole tread. Two layers under forefoot, 15 mm thick. Three layers under heel, 28 mm thick. Heel lift 13 mm. Heel width 83 mm.

This shoe, which was ranked number one by *Runner's World* in 1976, has long been my favorite for long distances. It seems to afford maximum cushioning and a great deal of comfort. Some runners find the toe box too shallow, but I have relatively small feet and toes and do not have this complaint. The shoe laces like a street shoe, with only four holes of lacing, a feature the manufacturer says helps reduce problems in the forefoot; I don't think it matters. Blucher lacing, which Dr. Gabriel highly recommends, provides a girdle effect for the sides of the foot and arch. Although Dr. Sheehan says this shoe lacks sufficient heel, I have not found it to be so. Dr. Weil thinks it may help relieve symptoms of Achilles tendinitis.

Nike LD-1000-V

New in 1977. Suggested price $39.95. Available in sizes 3–13 (up to E width). Single size-nine weighs 318.5 gm.

Upper. Polyester mesh with suede trim, gold and orange. U-box lacing. Padded ankle and heel collar.

Inside. Latex rubber sponge arch support. Spenco insole. Heel depth 71 mm. Ankle depth 47/46 mm. Toe box depth 22 mm.

Sole. Long waffle tread. Two layers under forefoot, 19 mm thick. Three layers under heel, 30 mm thick. Heel lift 11 mm. Heel width 80 mm.

This has another mesh upper that is great in summer, but cold in winter. The shoe gives me a feeling of flying, perhaps because it is light and has the marvelous waffle sole that cushions impact without adding much weight. I consider it a "class shoe," even though I twisted my ankle while running in a pair. It's another good shoe for runner's knee sufferers and those who have plantar fasciitis, according to Dr. Weil.

Nike Waffle Trainer

Introduced in 1975. Suggested price $27.95. Available in sizes 3–13 (up to E width). Single size-nine weighs 282.9 gm.

Upper. Oxford nylon with suede trim, blue and yellow. U-box lacing. Padded ankle and heel collar.

Inside. Latex rubber sponge arch support. Spenco insole. Heel depth 82 mm. Ankle depth 45/45 mm. Toe box 21 mm.

Sole. Waffle tread. Three layers under forefoot, 17 mm thick. Four layers under heel, 26 mm thick. Heel lift 9 mm. Heel width 79 mm.

This shoe is very much like the LD-1000-V, but with less heel flare and a solid nylon upper (not mesh). It is slightly lighter than the LD-1000-V, with some noticeable reduction in cushioning. I use the LD-1000-V for longer, slower distances, and I may use the Waffle Trainer to race in next season. With their quality materials and generally excellent workmanship, the Nike shoes offer a bit extra, I find. The company seems less inclined to cut corners than some others. Dr. Weil ranks this another shoe that may help soothe your runner's knee.

Puma Easy Rider

Introduced as new shoe in 1977. Suggested price $34.95. Available in sizes 3–13. Single size-nine weighs 402.3 gm.

Upper. Nylon with suede trim, white and blue. U-box lacing. Padded ankle and heel collar.

Inside. Latex foam cushion arch support. PVC foam, terry cloth insole. Heel depth 73 mm. Ankle depth 43/43 mm. Toe box depth 18 mm.

Sole. Stud-type tread. Two layers under forefoot, 17 mm thick. Three layers under heel, 28 mm thick. Heel lift 11 mm. Heel width 84 mm.

This is a lot of shoe, perhaps more than a small, light runner may need, but for the new, taller, or heavier jogger, I highly recommend it. I also find the Easy Rider the best shoe for snow and ice. Its stud-type tread gives excellent traction and the bulk of the shoe provides warmth and protection against surface irregularities.

One final word on shoes: Unless you are attempting to become a world-class runner, do not switch to the lower, lighter, less protective racing flats, even for races. Use a good training flat like Nikes or the New Balance 320. Racing flats are lower, more likely to strain your muscles and tendons, and your increased racing pace also produces extra strain—a combination that may very well cause shinsplints or Achilles tendinitis. In what appears to be a trend, several top finishers in recent races have been shod in the more protective training shoe rather than the racing flat.

5

Care and Feeding:
The Health of the Holistic Runner

The smoke of my own breath, . . .
My respiration and inspiration, the beating of
  my heart, the passing of blood and air through
  my lungs, . . .
The delight alone or in the risk of the street,
  or along the fields and hill-sides,
The feeling of health, the full-moon trill, the
  song of me rising from bed and meeting the sun.
                    From "Song of Myself"
                    by WALT WHITMAN

The great German coach, Ernst Van Aaken, is said to have taken overweight, poorly conditioned thirty-seven-year old Meinrad Nagale and, in a few years, made him a champion. At age forty six, Nagale ran a 2:29 marathon, finishing fourth in the World Veterans Championship. If this feat was not accomplished with mirrors, then how was it done? Nagale's answer: "Endurance training and special diet."

Fitness has other rewards for those of us uninterested in midlife acquisition of athletic trophies. Tom Osler, a former long-distance champion and now a coach and writer on conditioning, insists that "a properly conditioned runner whose body can handle even more than the daily training load is virtually injury and sickness proof." Kenneth Cooper suggests that symptoms of glaucoma, varicose veins, ulcers, and diabetes can be reduced by keeping fit. As already mentioned in Chapter One, Dr. Thomas Bassler, editor of the *American Medical Joggers Association Bulletin*, believes that a runner trained to run marathons is *immune* to heart attacks. Whether true or not, these pronouncements are titillating. However, one thing is certain. Higher stages of holistic running cannot be reached unless your body is prepared, and this preparation will improve the body's health. One has only to recall the Tarahumara Indians, who have been found to live longer than neighboring tribes, a fact that researchers attribute to their almost universal participation in long-distance running.

This chapter, therefore, offers some basic information that can help you run longer distances and stay fit. Most likely, your overall life style will improve, too, when you are fit, simply because you will be much healthier and possibly even happier. Getting down to specifics, a trained holistic runner on a sensible diet can expect that his or her body will experience:

> Increase in lean body mass
> Reduction of body fat
> Drop in heart rate
> Increase in amount of blood ejected at each heart stroke
> Increase in oxygen-carrying capacity of the blood
> Increase in efficiency with which the muscles extract oxygen from the blood
> Increase in blood supply and size of heart
> Reduction in level of circulating blood fats and stress hormones
> Decrease in stickiness of blood platelets, minimizing the risk of clots

In turn, these physical changes will influence your psyche, so that, as studies have demonstrated, you will also find that your:

Mood improves
Confidence increases
Depression lifts
Consciousness expands

There are three general areas that you must know something about in order to derive the foregoing benefits—that is, in order to maximize your ability to achieve holistic running and, simply, to feel better. These areas are 1) diet and nutrition, 2) the cardiovascular system, and 3) training.

Diet and Nutrition

Don't believe the skeptics who insist that weight loss cannot be achieved through exercise. What is absurd is to think that a radical diet, destined to be discarded after a brief period, can take—and keep—extra fat off your body. Holistic running, integrated into your life, will do more to make and keep you slim. The problem is that it does not happen quickly. Just as people disbelieve that holistic running leads to expanded awareness because it doesn't happen overnight, they will scorn the idea that long-distance running is a good weight reducer, for the same reason. A beginner must be able to run several miles each session to achieve even the first stages of holistic running, and this process takes several months. Even after you are running twenty-five miles or more per week, your running program is not likely to result in a significant weight change for three to six months.

According to Professor Jack H. Wilmore, chairman of the Department of Physical Education at the University of Arizona, when you run you lose body fat and *gain* lean body mass. Fat weight is all the fat on your body, while lean weight is everything else: bone, muscle, blood and so on. In the first six months of running, expect to gain from five to seven pounds of lean body weight, especially—as you would expect—in the legs. Although the scale will not provide much evidence of virtue during this period, your pants or skirts should, because your shape will be changing. I find that friends who go into long-distance running and stick with it almost invariably have their clothes taken in or replaced *before* any dramatic weight loss is recorded by the scale. In my case, my waist diminished so significantly that I had to trade my belts for suspenders. Now I'm not at the mercy of a tailor every time my girth contracts another notch.

Exercise is a more gradual but also more effective way to lose weight than trendy radical diets, which lead to abrupt, but temporary, weight losses. It is impossible to lose more than two and a half pounds of *fat* per week, even on a starvation diet. Anyone who claims to be losing more is in fact reporting loss of body fluids, which are replaced when you drink a glass of water. You should know, furthermore, that diets that lead to dehydration can be extremely harmful.

When I got my first driver's license at the age of sixteen, I weighed twenty pounds more than I do today at thirty-eight. Almost all the extra pounds were shed after I began running. Compare my experience to that of the average American, who, according to

Professor Wilmore, tends to add one pound of body weight per year from the age of twenty-five. Not only is he gaining fat weight, but he is simultaneously *losing* lean body mass at the rate of approximately a half pound per year. This means that he will have gained thirty pounds by the time he is age fifty-five, but, even more distressing, he will have gained forty-five pounds of fat. And the situation is not improving. In December 1977, the National Center for Health Statistics reported that American men and women are *more* overweight than they were a decade earlier. The average man weights 20 to 30 pounds more than he ought to, and four pounds more than he did ten years earlier; the average woman weighs fifteen to thirty pounds too much, and one pound more than a decade ago.

Of all exercises, running seems best suited for stimulating weight loss. The average male carries about 15 percent body fat at twenty-one, while the average female at that age carries 25 percent body fat. At forty-five, the average male will have increased his body fat by approximately 25 percent, and the average female will be about 20 percent fatter. But male *runners* tend to reach an optimal weight at which they carry from 6 to 14 percent body fat, and women *runners* tend to carry approximately 15 to 19 percent fat.

So running evidently works very efficiently to burn your body fat. This is demonstrated in the following chart, in which Philip K. Wilson, executive director of the Cardiac Rehabilitation Program at the University of Wisconsin—La Crosse illustrates how long it takes to burn off the hundred and five calories in an eight-ounce glass of Coca-Cola through four different activities:

Walking	20 minutes
Bicycling	18 minutes
Swimming	12 minutes
Jogging	11 minutes

This chart ought to suggest another critical fact. If you eat too much, you can't possibly run it all off. For example, if you have one glass of beer, which contains a hundred thirty to a hundred forty calories, it will take you a mile and a half to two miles of jogging to run it off. To get rid of the effects of a four-ounce glass of champagne, which contains eighty-five calories, you must add eight or nine minutes to your run. One glass of vermouth is a hundred seventy calories and will take eighteen minutes to burn up.

It becomes obvious that to lose weight, you must eat less. The sacrifice is not too grave. If you currently eat two pieces of bread with butter at each meal, you are consuming 600 to 700 calories, which would take you a full hour to run off. Why not try staying away from the bread? Or, to put the intake problem another way, there are approximately 3,000 to 3,500 calories in one pound of body weight. You can gain a pound per year, by eating only one extra 10-calorie potato chip each day. Conversely, you will stay free of that fat if, every day, you forego that potato chip or its equivalent. Most of us eat too much, anyway. The average American consumes, on the average, 1,353 pounds of food per year, or 3.71 pounds per day. That's 1.2 million calories per year, or 3,293 a day—enough to sustain a 190-pound lumberjack or construction worker, or a moderately active 220-pound weekend athlete. In contrast, a good runner requires only 2,500 calories to run a *marathon*.

Eating less combined with long-distance running

will not only reduce your weight, but improve your shape as well, since, when you run, that extra fat is converted into lean body mass. Don't be misled by cynics who argue that the more you run, the more you will have to eat. Most runners find that a good run has a dampening effect on their appetites, and although scientific explanations of this phenomenon differ, they do seem to confirm that a strenuous workout has the effect of suppressing appetite.

Dieters get another premium if they achieve holistic running. Physiologists claim that the difference between the number of calories burned at a jogger's nine-minute-per-mile pace and that burned at a fast six-minute-per-mile run is insignificant. Nevertheless, those who run long distances, bringing their bodies close to the point of maximum effort, will continue to burn calories at an increased rate for some time *after* their run ends. This occurs because calories are burned at a rate consistent with the body's metabolism, and after a strenuous run, the metabolic rate remains elevated and takes several hours to return to normal.

Bill Rodgers eats three good meals a day and sleeps ten hours each night. In addition, according to *Sports Illustrated*, he rises each night around 3:00 A.M. for a fourth meal of apricot nectar mixed with flat ginger ale, quarts of cola, chocolate chip cookies, and mayonnaise, which he takes straight from the jar with a tablespoon. When he is getting ready for a marathon, Rodgers runs a hundred seventy miles a week, so we can understand his nocturnal indulgences. The rest of us must be more austere.

I eat less and I eat different foods since I began to run long distances. There are several reasons. When you run you are in touch with your body, and holistic running, in particular, expands awareness, including awareness of your insides. The morning after I eat a big steak for dinner, my body tells me that it is dense and heavy. It's not much fun to run when you feel that way. At an evening meeting or dinner party, I used to drink one or two martinis. But I found that running was almost impossible the morning after. So with no systematic plan—my diet has gradually shifted:

> From heavy meats to fish and poultry
> From hard liquor to wine
> From heavy desserts to fruits and cheese
> From big lunches to salads and yogurt
> From bacon and eggs to whole-grain cereals

I stopped smoking cigarettes before I began running, but still indulge in an occasional cigar. Because cigarettes are inhaled, your lungs will naturally resist them as you progress in holistic running. Even if you can't stop smoking cold turkey, running will improve your health. Running helps to break down the toxic hemoglobin affixed to carbon dioxide, which is especially prevalent in the blood of smokers. Even if you smoke, your ability to exchange oxygen and carbon dioxide in the blood will be enhanced.

A sensible diet for an athlete is no different than anyone else's sensible diet, according to Dr. Nathan J. Smith, who wrote *Food for Sport*. Meatless diets can support an active exercise program, as long as sources of protein such as rice, beans, nuts, and grains are eaten in proper combinations. The "Zen macrobiotic diet" has nothing to do with Zen or yoga and will not sustain anyone, be he or she athletic or indolent. It lacks most vitamins and the critically necessary mineral, iron.

Athletes, incidentally, tend to be vitamin freaks. Many trainers will recommend supplementation of the B vitamins, and vitamins C and E. But, according to David L. Costill of the Human Performance Laboratory at Ball State University, popping vitamin pills is probably unnecessary. It is true that B-complex vitamins, especially thiamine, play an important role in the metabolism of fats and carbohydrates, and that exercise may cause the body to consume fifteen times more thiamine than when it is inactive. But it does not necessarily follow that runners should take vitamin B supplements. If you are not simultaneously involved in a significant campaign to lose weight while you increase your running program, you are probably getting enough vitamin B from your regular diet. (Protein foods and whole grains are excellent sources.)

Vitamin C is thought to increase the blood's oxygen-carrying capacity, which if true, could make greater amounts of oxygen available to the muscles. But, so far, studies relating improved physical performance to vitamin C supplements have been inconclusive. David Costill thinks there is not sufficient reason for the long distance runner to carry a necklace of vitamin C pills with him, although it is still too early to reject the possibility that this vitamin may be important.

As for vitamin E, normal daily food intake provides more than enough of it. (It is especially abundant in vegetable oils, whole grains, and eggs.) Professor Costill believes it is unlikely that the taking of E supplements is justified, although studies do show that the running endurance performance of middle-aged men is improved when their diets are supplemented with wheat germ oil, which is high in vitamin E, as well as other nutrients. All in all, Costill concludes that "popping vitamin pills is a rather expensive way to increase the vitamin content of the urine." Sensible athletes do not make a fetish out of vitamins. The legendary coach Arthur Lydiard, who trained dozens of world-class New Zealand runners, recommends vitamin supplements, but only "as sort of an insurance policy against injury and staleness." He adds: "Taking vitamin and mineral tablets certainly won't do us any harm—in moderation." Runner Bill Rodgers agrees: "The few vitamins I take are the ones that can't hurt you if you take too many of them, and I don't take much: one multivitamin a day and 500 milligrams of vitamin C."

The Cardiovascular System

The running rage has spread far and wide the story of the first marathon runner, now everyone knows that in 490 B.C. Pheidippides ran all the way from Marathon, carrying news of the Athenians' victory over the Persians back to Athens, whereupon he died on the spot. We don't know what he died of. Assuming it was a heart attack, though, he apparently did not know what Dr. Tom Bassler would declare, almost 2,500 years later: No one capable of running a marathon can have a fatal heart attack. Unfortunately for Pheidippides, he seems to have proved the opposite—that an untrained runner can kill himself in a marathon.

The cardiovascular benefit of running is best understood when dealing with less extreme distances. The American Medical Joggers Association has sensibly said that a running program consistent with the early stages of holistic running—six miles, or one hour, every other day—provides "some" cardiovascular protection. Yet there are, from time to time, cases like that of Dr. David W. Cloos, who died at age thirty while jogging on Martha's Vineyard, soon after having a physical examination that included a "normal" electrocardiogram.

If you are over thirty-five, you must think about your heart. You might also think about the mutable factors that are apparently causing a decline in the cardiovascular death rate. In 1975, despite an increasingly older and larger population, the total number of deaths in the United States from cardiovascular diseases dropped to below one million for the first time since 1967. Doctors attribute the decline to several factors: a reduction in the consumption of saturated fats and cholesterol, a decline in the consumption of tobacco, better diagnosis and treatment of high blood pressure, and the explosion in exercise programs such as long-distance running. Supporting this conclusion further is evidence that the death rate from cardiovascular disease continues to go up in countries where similar changes in personal habits are not taking place, like England and Norway.

In November, 1977, one of these factors, vigorous exercise, was linked scientifically to cardiovascular protection. Dr. Ralph Paffenbarger, Jr., of Stanford University School of Medicine, studied seventeen thousand Harvard alumni and found a protective effect among those who participated in intense physical activity for at least three hours a week, expending a total of two thousand or more calories a week through exercise. According to this study, lesser amounts of exercise produced no measurable benefits in terms of reducing risk of heart attack.

Believe it or not, this was the first study that established a real link between exercise and the prevention of heart attacks. Until this research was published, the active role of exercise in the prevention of heart attacks was merely presumed. This study also decimated a common myth promoted by the sedentary cynic—that exercise benefits only those who are fit to begin with. Dr. Paffenbarger found that the alumni who were varsity athletes as students were not protected against heart disease in their adult years unless they maintained a high level of physical activity. In contrast, men who were not athletes while in college demonstrated a reduced risk of heart disease if they took up strenuous activities later in life.

If you remain unconvinced, contemplate the growing number of heart attack victims who are now thriving as they participate in rehabilitation programs emphasizing long-distance running. One of the most ambitious programs for such individuals is Dr. Terence Kavanagh's Toronto Rehabilitation Centre. Dr. Kavanagh has large numbers of patients who have suffered heart attacks and now jog between fifty to eighty miles per week. Twenty of his protégés with histories of heart attack have run in more than fifty marathons, and one of them ran a marathon only fifteen months after suffering his heart attack.

Here are the actual figures which show what happens to your cardiovascular system when you become a long-distance runner.

Lower Heart Rate

The average person has a resting heart rate of 65 beats per minute. A world-class runner averages 47 beats per minute, while a good runner averages 51 beats, and a fit amateur between 55 and 60. Such lower figures mean that the heart is operating more efficiently.

Higher Stroke Volume

During a hard workout, the runner raises his heart rate to 75 to 80 percent of its maximum. The maximum heart rate tends to be about 220 beats per minute, less the age of the runner, although recent studies suggest that all fit runners, regardless of speed or age, tend to have an average maximum heart rate of around 197 beats per minute. In order to maximize the flow at which the blood can deliver oxygen to the muscles and remove carbon dioxide, the runner's heart gradually increases the volume of blood it can pump with each stroke. (To accomplish this, the heart itself may thicken, like any other muscle that is exercised.) Even at rest, the efficient heart rate of a runner is lower than that of a sedentary person, because, with each stroke, more blood is delivered to the body.

Increased Volume of High-Density Lipoproteins

Recent studies have indicated that there are two kinds of blood lipids, or lipoproteins. The low-density kind are found in cholesterol and silt up your arteries as they precipitate. High-density lipids (HDL's) on the other hand, seem to be able to prevent cholesterol from being deposited there and to flush away much of the residue. Dr. Ronald Lawrence, the president and founder of the American Medical Joggers Association, reports that AMJA members who competed in the 1977 Boston marathon were found to have enhanced levels of HDL's in their bloodstreams when they were tested in Boston a day before the race.

Improved Oxygen Consumption

In the sedentary person, maximal oxygen consumption decreases with age, but long-distance runners do not evidence the same decline. In fact Dr. Noel D. Nequin, medical director of the Cardiac Rehabilitation Center of Swedish Covenant Hospital in Chicago, says that running may delay the onset of decreased oxygen consumption by twenty years. Far from decreasing, the runner's ability to obtain and utilize oxygen, or, in other words, to function aerobically, is enhanced. As for those who have low oxygen-consumption rates, they will more quickly run out of oxygen when performing stressful tasks. Then their body will produce lactic acid and an anaerobic condition will set in.

Increased Ability of the Muscles to Extract Oxygen from the Blood

The density of capillaries in muscles used in running, such as in the calf, has been known to increase 100 percent in response to long-distance training. The content of myoglobin in the muscles is what determines how much oxygen will be taken from its carrier, the blood hemoglobin. Long-distance running is said to increase the myoglobin content of the muscles by 200 percent.

All of this sounds terrific, but remember:

The Greek runner Pheidippides died when he arrived in Athens.

E. M. Forster's Harold achieved an athlete's true goal, "the mystic state," and promply died.

Jim Shettler, a first-class long-distance runner, died on a long, slow workout.

Dr. David Cloos, age thirty, collapsed and died while jogging on Martha's Vineyard.

Presumably, each of these athletes—mythical, fictional, and real—died because some component of his respective cardiovascular system went on the fritz. Dr. Cloos had just had a checkup and an electrocardiogram. What he apparently had not had, however, was an *exercise stress test*.

The American College of Sports Medicine recommends a stress test every eighteen months for runners over thirty years of age and every year for those forty and older. This elaborate but important examination can identify cardiovascular problems and diagnose their cause. Dr. Cloos passed a standard physical examination, but might have been forewarned of a problem had he undertaken a stress test. Perhaps the most important function of a good exercise stress test is to help you determine your capacity for strenuous exercise. There are various procedures for the test, but the most useful for a person involved in or contemplating running puts you through several increasingly rigorous periods of exercise on a treadmill. Blood pressure readings and an electrocardiogram are recorded every minute, beginning at rest, then when you peak at near-maximum physiological limits, as well as during the recovery period. Maximum oxygen consumption is also measured, to help determine your optimum capacity for aerobic exercise.

An exercise stress test is useful in two ways, according to Dr. Nequin: "It will tell the experienced runner how fit he or she *really* is. Also, it may uncover significant coronary disorders which may not be accompanied by any obvious symptoms."

Like any other test, the stress test is imperfect. It can indicate a serious problem when none is apparent, but it can also fail to indicate a serious problem that does exist. Nevertheless, if you are forty or older, it is without doubt the best known means of assuring yourself that an attempt to expand your consciousness to encompass the world through holistic running won't endanger your health.

Training

It is not an insignificant fact that the first man to break the four-minute mile was a student of medicine. Roger Bannister's professional background gave him two important advantages. First, he could develop a training program based upon the most sophisticated information then available about human physiology. Second, he knew how to exploit the extraordinary potential of the human body without destroying it. Yet even those of us not destined to shatter records can improve our holistic workouts with some basic training information. The following section, which is divided into two parts, is designed for that purpose. The first discusses regular workouts that can be sustained through the year. (I assume that the holistic runner will generally want to cover thirty to forty miles per week.) The second, will examine the adjustments in training that you will want to make in order to prepare for a race.

Regular Workouts: Warm-Up/Workout/Cool-down

Every workout should consist of warm-up, work-out, and cool-down. Everybody agrees that a warm-up is essential before shifting into high gear, to insure that your muscles and tendons are not so stiff as to hazard injuries, and that your cardiovascular system is moving the oxygen-rich blood around your body with some efficiency. But everybody does *not* agree on what form a warm-up should take. Some prescribe ten to fifteen minutes of yoga and other stretching exercises—a prelude that no one thinks could possibly be harmful. But others, including Dr. Sheehan and me, substitute a slow jog as warm-up. Dr. Sheehan runs his best workouts at an average of six to seven minutes per mile, but he runs his warm-up mile at a ten-minute pace. It takes between three to ten minutes for a sweat to begin rising—for second wind to come. This means that a slow first mile gives your heart and respiratory rates a chance to adapt to the run; after this warm-up period, they stop rising and even begin to taper off.

Then you can begin your holistic workout. For the most part, you should gradually approach the greatest speed and maximum distance at which you can run "aerobically." An aerobic workout is sustained on the oxygen you can take in, and so it does not result in the body having to repay an "oxygen debt." In an aerobic workout, your body is not compelled to burn its own fuel, its fat or muscle, and lactic acid is not deposited in the muscles. Consequently, the holistic runner can continue the workout for a long period and continue to build up, rather than break down, his body.

As you work out, check your heart rate from time to time. For a holistic run you will want to stay below your maximum anaerobic heart rate of roughly 220 beats per minute less your age. Depending on your level of conditioning, a maximum aerobic heart rate of 130 to 150 should see you through a run.

Long, slow distance training is the preferred workout, especially for holistic runners. Such continuous runs will minimize your chances of incurring stress-related injuries. In general, you are better off timing the workout, rather than measuring the distance you cover. For example, when I travel, I bring along an old stopwatch. I have no way of measuring distance on my morning run, but I carry the watch and run for at least one hour. Workouts should be pleasant, and slow. Whether you are running alone or in company, a good way to gauge your pace is whether you can be convivial and chat with fellow runners. If your breath is too labored for conviviality, you are going too fast.

There has been some scientific demonstration of the addictive quality of holistic training. Dr. Frederick Borkeland wanted to make a study of the effects on daily runners of one month of exercise deprivation, but he couldn't get *any* daily runners to give running up for the sake of science! He had to settle for runners who ran an average of three times a week. In these runners, he found that the month's layoff resulted in impaired sleep, increased sexual tension, and an increased need on the part of the runners to be with others. This last finding could be interpreted to mean that the runners had lost their holistic self-awareness during the layoff and were compensating with conventional Western reinforcement.

Race Training

If you want to increase your endurance or speed, and, especially, if you care to try a race or two, you should occasionally vary long, slow workouts with shorter, more intense ones. All good runners who enjoy racing spend one or more days a week in what is called *fartlek* (a Swedish word for speed play) or "interval" training. In *fartlek*, the runner experiments by doing part of his workout at a relatively slow pace and the rest at greater speeds. He will run measured intervals in a prescribed time, rest a prescribed time, and then run the same distance again, at the same or a better speed. These training methods increase neuromuscular strength and coordination; they also increase endurance, training the body to perform efficiently in an anaerobic state, when the effort is greater than the body's ability to burn oxygen. In long-distance races, the body must rely on stored energy, and interval training helps prepare for this.

Everyone should set his own goals for interval training. Frank Shorter runs intervals equal to his shortest competitive events, around five thousand meters. He attempts in each interval to equal or break his best time, which is pretty close to world-record time. From the sublime to the ridiculous: Occasionally I try to run one-mile intervals. My best time for the mile is just under six minutes, which is a minute slower than Shorter's *average* time for a whole marathon. But you get the idea. I find an occasional interval workout on the track is fun; it stretches different muscles and makes my next few holistic runs all the better.

Remember that you are not under a sergeant's or guru's orders to work out every day. Too many potential holistic runners drop out because they make themselves feel anxious or guilty every time life's obligations or plain laziness keeps them from their daily run. Thirty or forty minutes of running five times a week will provide you with enough "aerobic points" to make Dr. Cooper happy, even if you can't thereby achieve an advanced stage of holistic running. The following running schedule, which is based on my own, is proposed for the holistic runner in fair condition. It will provide you with thirty-five miles a week of running as well as two days off for other exercise or just sitting around.

SUNDAY. A long, slow run of ten miles. You are not under pressure to get anywhere, so take it easy and enjoy it.

MONDAY. Eight miles at a slightly faster pace, to achieve higher holistic levels in fewer miles and minutes, and to increase your endurance.

TUESDAY. Off. Try some yoga or other stretching and strengthening exercises today.

WEDNESDAY. Intervals. Jog one ten-minute mile. Then try four six-minute miles, making sure your pulse returns to 160 or below before each successive one.

THURSDAY. Six miles at an easy pace. Feel how refreshing this run will be after your interval workout.

FRIDAY. Off. Make sure you are stretching those gravity muscles.

SATURDAY. Six miles will give you a week's total of thirty-five, but go further if you feel like it.

Don't forget the cool-down. When you stop running, the body takes a while to adjust. In the meantime, blood continues to be delivered in volume to your legs. If you stop cold, it may pool there, causing various problems, including fainting. Also, lactic acid may accumulate in your muscles, causing soreness and muscle cramps, unless you help to get rid of it by jogging and walking through a short cool-down.

Overdoing It

Western jocks, unlike prudent yogas, tend to excess. Don't. Over-exertion provides no benefits. It brings on nothing but aches and pains.

If you experience chest pains, nausea, lightheadedness, extreme breathlessness, or vomiting, stop. And if the symptoms do not quickly subside, go to a doctor immediately. Heat stroke, incidentally, can kill you, so don't run at high noon on hot days. Stop any time you feel overheated or experience nausea or diarrhea. Never work out if your temperature is above normal. There have been many cases of runners who have died by not taking this precaution. While the specific causes of death remain unknown, researchers say that the infection causing the fever can quickly reach your heart and produce an inflammation of the heart muscle, what is known as myocarditis. When combined with heavy exercise, this condition can be deadly. Realizing the importance of caution, Dr. Roger Bannister insists on two training rules: 1. Training and conditioning must be stopped during periods of fever, and 2. after returning to workouts, start gradually and listen and feel for what your body tells you about limits. Don't overdo it.

As a rule, do not work out within two to four hours of eating a meal. Light easy-to-digest food apparently does not have an adverse effect, but it won't give you any significant advantage, either. One reason I enjoy early-morning runs is because of the minimal risk of abdominal complications from any of the day's indulgences.

Liquid refreshment, on the other hand, is desperately important in long-distance running. Always drink several glasses of water before a workout and stop for water or other liquid along the way. Your liquid requirements while running will depend on the heat and humidity. High heat and humidity will result in maximum dehydration due to sweating, whereas a cold day with cloud cover and a breeze will minimize the problem. In the winter, dehydration isn't a problem for me, even though I drink nothing on cold winter days *during* runs of from twelve to fifteen miles. However, I drink five or six small cups of water *before* starting.

Most doctors and trainers don't recommend the special runners' concoctions, such as Gatorade, which tend to be high in glucose concentration and therefore restrict the speed at which the fluids can be cleared through the body. If you like these drinks, dilute them with equal parts of water to minimize the problem. The lack of any nutritional value in water is not considered a problem. Apparently, a runner can get by on water alone during races of up to fifty and a hundred miles in length.

When the weather is warm, don't wait to feel thirsty before starting to take liquids during your workout. Your thirst gauge will be inadequate to determine your need, so drink in excess of your thirst. If you are in a race, it is best to stop and take a full cup

of water every three to five miles. Never pass up a refreshment table in a race. Dehydration causes more
dropouts in marathons than any other problem.

For a long time it was believed that alcohol was the
worst possible kind of liquid to consume in workouts
and races, because it immobilizes the enzymes involved
in glycogen conversion for up to twelve hours after
imbibing. Oxygen is wasted on these inactive enzymes,
and the runner was thought to be less efficient as a
result. Times are changing, though. Dr. Bassler, who
runs twenty-five miles each Sunday and drinks a beer
every few miles, says he "jogs a six pack" per Sunday.
Dick Walsh of Las Vegas, at the age of fifty-four, had
never run better than a 3:27 marathon. The night before the 1977 Boston Marathon, he consumed six beers
(and a pizza) before midnight. The next day, he
drank a beer at the nine-mile mark and another at the
seventeen-mile mark. "I was a child while running," he
says. "I stopped at least four times to hug a child or to
chat with a girl. I finished with a great euphoria, suffering no hurts whatsoever, in a time of 3:17."

Dr. Sheehan has become a convert, too. He ran the
Boston on four bummed beers, and I saw him line up
at the start of the First Chicago Distance Classic with
can in hand. He says that beer works because it is a
food, as well as a drug, providing seven calories per
gram. And these calories don't need to be digested because alcohol goes right through the wall of the stomach and small intestine. "So at blood levels below
two hundred milligrams, a level that impairs heart action," he says, "alcohol is fine. Two beers an hour can
provide a stimulus and a potent source of ready calories." On the other hand there *is* a limit. Dr. Sheehan
drank six beers one Saturday night, then ran a good
six-mile workout the next day. After a day off, he

drank another six beers in the evening. Result: "The next day I thought about running but went home and took a three-hour nap instead."

Carbohydrate Loading

Remember that, to some extent, holistic running depends on increasing the amount of nutrients, especially glycogen, received by the brain. So, even if you choose not to race, but simply wish to improve your holistic running, there may be ways to increase your energy level by changing your diet. Oxygen, of course, cannot be stored, but it is the main source of initial energy for running. After oxygen is depleted, the body turns to its major energy storage components, glycogen first and then fats. Long-distance running tires you mainly because it depletes your store of glycogen.

A form of carbohydrate, glycogen is made up of sugar molecules arranged in a polymer, which is a group of molecules linked together in a specific fashion. It is stored in the muscles and, as required, passed into the muscles through the metabolic process. Racing, or day after day of holistic running, drastically uses up the glycogen stores in your muscles. After two or three days at ten miles each day, muscle glycogen is reduced to near zero, and it may take days to restore it to preworkout levels.

Many racers "carbohydrate-load" before a race to maximize the glycogen available during the race. This elaborate ritual first requires several days of carbohydrate depletion, during which the runner is training hard and eating protein-rich, low-carbohydrate foods. Then three or four days before the race, he begins less strenuous workouts, at the same time eating foods that are high in glycogen-carrying carbohydrates, like spaghetti and bread. The value of the "depletion" phase of the procedure is controversial, but most runners tend to eat carbohydrate-rich food, at least on the day before the race.

Whether you race or not, holistic runs at near-peak performance will probably use up your glycogen stores. One way to tell is to weigh yourself. If you weigh significantly less after a run, you may have depleted your glycogen stores. Because water is sequestered in the body with glycogen, a loss of water will usually mean a loss of glycogen as well. So, to some extent, the holistic runner is justified in indulging a fancy for starchy foods. My favorite glycogen-building evening meal, especially on the day before a race, is spaghetti with a bland sauce, lots of good French or Italian bread, apple pie, and beer. How satisfying that discipline and desire occasionally demand the same of us!

Protection from the Elements

The only important thing runners need to remember is to wear the minimum that is necessary to allow good ventilation of body heat and prevent frostbite. Less is more, in this regard. On hot days, running shorts and a T-shirt or singlet are all that should be worn. Don't try to lose extra weight by overdressing. All you will lose is body fluid through sweat, and you will risk heat stroke into the bargain. Don't try to wrap up in an extra set of sweat clothes to "sweat out" a cold. As we saw, evidence is accumulating to the effect that you can thus bring on myocarditis, a secondary heart infection that can be fatal.

I have recently become enamored of nylon shorts and singlets. They're light and facilitate the drying of sweat better than cotton. They're also easier to maintain. When I return from my run, I get into the shower while still dressed, peel shorts and singlet off under the water, and give them a rinse. Nylon dries fast and is good for travel, too. As for socks, I recommend always wearing good socks that have carefully machined seams to minimize blisters. Socks mainly woven from quality cotton, with some acrylic or nylon added, seem to work best. As pointed out before, tube socks tend to wrinkle and cause blisters. In the hottest weather, I like low-cut socks that just fit the shoes.

In the winter, I run even when the wind-chill factor is − 70 degrees Fahrenheit. My only problems have involved failure adequately to protect my hands and—if the truth must be known—penis. However, none of these appendages has ever suffered more than the slight stiffening and discomfort symptomatic of incipient, but not serious, frostbite. I have no serious problems in this weather when I wear long underwear, cotton running shorts, a sweat suit, light cotton mittens under down-filled ski mittens, a knitted wool cap, and a ski mask with no opening except for the eyes. (After my first experience with incipient penile frostbite, a friend offered to construct a mink-lined jock strap, but so far she has not come through.) My feet never seem to get too cold, though I do switch from cotton to wool socks in the depths of winter, and I stay away from open mesh shoes. The Puma Easy Rider, with its flared, cleated sole and solid nylon upper, makes an excellent winter running shoe. When the wind is at its worst and the rain and snow cut into me, I add a light nylon shirt or windbreaker. This really seals me in. In fact, it can easily cause overheating and is rarely necessary.

A runner who runs near Chicago tells me he has divided winter into "one-mitten" and "two-mitten" days. When the temperature is brisk but not frigid, he wears a mitten on one hand until the other gets cold. Then he switches. After a mile or so, he switches back. Why not wear mittens on both hands simultaneously? "Because then my hands would get too hot." Of course, on the coldest days he wears both.

Don't worry about the frigid air searing your lungs. That's largely an old wives' tale. The lungs receive air warmed by the mouth and throat and, in my case, by a closed ski mask as well. Cardiac patients are advised to take it easier in very cold weather, since the body is obviously under more stress then. And if the wind is high, you will enjoy yourself more if you head into the wind at first and come home with it at your back.

Some runners, myself included, find that they experience chafing in certain spots, such as the nipples and crotch area. Cramer makes a skin ointment for athletes that seems a bit thicker and therefore longer lasting than ordinary petroleum jelly; a touch of its "Skin-Lube" on these areas prevents any problem. I also use it on my feet to reduce friction around the areas most susceptible to calluses and blisters. Some runners, again including me, cover their feet entirely with Vasoline before a race. This seems to minimize risk of blisters, overheated feet, and other problems associated with friction.

Finally, you may want some guidance as to the best time of day to run. The answer is that only you can decide that. I know holistic runners who cannot work out except at dawn. Count me among them (although yoga and calisthenics are easier for me in the evening). Others are noon people, while many others are consistently out in the evening. There are two relevant factors: life style and body functions. Every person is on a different schedule. I like the early morning because 1) it is beautiful, 2) it is quiet, 3) there are no distractions, and 4) I lose little time from the rest of my life. At lunch I often have meetings. If I ran in the evening, I would see even less of my family and friends. Also, I am certain that my metabolism and other body functions favor early morning runs, just as the same considerations favor noon runs for Dr. Sheehan, and evening runs for others. Body functions, including hormone production and physical performance, differ significantly among people. Dr. Cooper notes that morning runners statistically seem to *persist* better than others. But, really, I run in the morning because—when I am finished—I can live the day more fully.

6

Racing with Myself:
I Win One for the Fearful Kid

> On action alone be thy interest, never on its fruits;
> Let not the fruits of action be thy motive,
> Nor be thy attachment to inaction.
> Holding pleasure and pain alike,
> Gain and loss, victory and defeat,
> Then gird thyself for battle:
> Thus thou shalt not get evil.
>
> From the *Bhagavad-Gita*.

Race day. Up at 5:00 A.M. A nervous glance out the window to check the weather. Crazy to schedule a twenty-kilometer race in Chicago in July. The sky looks like a pale overcast, but who can tell when the sun is still invisible, only hinting that dawn will soon arrive? No rain. Must pray that the clouds will keep the July heat off the lakefront until the race is over, but not release the rain, either. I start a form of yoga breathing: belly expands as air rushes in to the count of four. Belly contractions to push it out at the same rate.

Four glasses of water interrupt the choreography of my breath. I started drinking lots of liquid yesterday, when I met Dr. Joan Ullyot, who is here for today's run. Even if she had not gotten her M.D. degree from Harvard, been a formidable marathon runner, and author of one of the best books on running, I would still have taken her advice to heart. If she had told me to eat laundry starch or lead-based paint, I probably would have done so, because she is very attractive and very convincing. Instead, she was belting down water and advised me to do the same, and continue to do so until and on into tomorrow's race. She also urged me to have my favorite dinner of spaghetti with bland sauce, lots of bread, and apple pie. All of this in the interest of maximizing my high-energy glycogen reservoir for the race. Boston and New York–marathon winner Bill Rodgers wonders: "[Do] I run high mileage so I can eat like this, or do I eat like this so I can run high mileage?"

I unroll my exercise mat and begin to limber up. Early morning is the most painful time for stretching exercises. Muscles have been happily asleep, asking no blood and receiving none. Tight and dry, my neck, shoulders, back, thighs, calves, and Achilles tendons resist the tugging as I touch my toes, as I then lean into the wall for "wall push-ups," then lie supine, raising my trunk off the mat and forcing it down toward my outstretched, complaining legs. Next, I fold my legs back against my chest until the knees touch. Gradually, blood begins to trickle into my muscles, the small of my back uncurls and molds to the mat, my body feels less like lumber and more like flesh.

By now I am able to attempt my favorite stretching exercise, the leg-over or *halasana* (the plough), described earlier in Chapter Four. On my back, I raise legs and trunk straight above, then bring the legs back behind my head. Gradually, I lower them until they touch the mat. At first I force them to remain there only ten seconds or so before bringing them up a few inches so I can breathe and my muscles and tendons can relax. Then down again for another ten seconds, fighting the resistance in my neck, shoulders, back, and legs. My feet begin to tremble as if palsied. By the third time, my body's resistance to this pretzel-like posture begins to diminish. I begin a three- or four-minute spell in this position, breathing restored to a deep four count in, four out. I feel the tensions in my neck and shoulders loosen. I stretch my legs straighter. I am in a mild trance.

Because it is race day, the interlude of exercise is over when I unroll from the *halasana*. Otherwise, there would be muscle-strengthening curls, push-ups, leg-ups, and my muscle-stretching routine.

With profound relief, I find that the water, breathing, and exercise have accomplished one essential purpose, at least. I grab a magazine and dash off to the bathroom. Of course, the race sponsor, the First National Bank of Chicago, will provide many portable toilets near the starting line in the alley behind the bank building, but those cramped plastic outhouses are hardly conducive to prerace composure, especially after waiting in long lines of nervous runners.

So far so good. Another glance out the window reveals cloud cover holding well: a mild morning. The race begins at 8:00 A.M., so I will not eat breakfast, though many entrants will be putting away pancakes or oatmeal right now. Instead, I have another couple of pints of water and a warm defizzed Coke. Frank Shorter will have a banana before he starts. Later, I will see Dr. Sheehan at the starting line, swilling his usual can of beer.

Although I have been running for years, I never entered a race before this year. Why, I would ask my friends who raced, would I want to pervert a satisfying and refreshing aspect of my life by forcing it into a rigid set of obligatory routines? Racing involves competition, which, I would say, is pernicious. It means that I would have to vandalize my lovely, lyrical morning runs, turn them into dogged training sessions. The rest of my life is filled with obligations and responsibilities. If running descends to the same level, if it becomes another chore, I'll likely give it up. And anyhow, I would always sheepishly conclude, "I ain't fast enough."

My colleague George Vernon, a veteran of the Boston marathon, finally seduced me into racing. On business trips, as we ran together from hotels through downtown streets of Atlanta, Houston, and Philadelphia, he talked of ritual and ceremony, of fellowship and fun, of motivation and inspiration. "Solitary running is why we do it," he said but added that once in a while it was exhilarating to see hundreds, even thousands, of other solitary runners come together. He told me racing can help develop pride in one's own performance and urged me to try it. "Win—without beating someone," George said.

I decided to sign up for a couple of races to see how I liked it. As I'd feared, sometimes the extra workouts seemed too much like work. On the other hand, it was useful to have a simple goal around which to organize them. And later, I found that I had no trouble returning to a less demanding, unstructured running schedule.

George promised that I would be as fast as half the entrants in any open race. And in my first, a ten-miler, damned if I didn't finish 443rd out of 863, almost exactly in the middle. So here I am again, dressed in running clothes and warm-up suit, carrying my ditty bag replete with sweatbands, towels, tape, Vaseline, postrace tea blended with orange juice, and assorted charms. I pick up George, drive downtown, and park near the finish line, on the lakefront at Buckingham Fountain.

A crew is setting up the display of trophies for the winner and those who will finish first in each class. I do not covet these prizes. I am not in it for the gold plate. Anyway there isn't the slightest chance of my placing. The trophies, nevertheless, rivet my attention. "Racing," wrote Roger Bannister, "leads to the most remarkable self-discovery." The trophies evoke a strong string of memories. . . .

I am very small and we are living in an apartment on the northwest side of the city. Bookshelves are built into the wall on either side of the living room fireplace. A few books are scattered there, but most of the shelves groan under the weight of bowling trophies, scores of them. My father was an athlete. As a kid, he played basketball at Hull House. At Crane Technical High School, he was a small but fast halfback. Later, he played for and managed semiprofessional baseball teams for industrial leagues. Sometimes his team would play one game in the morning, drive madly to another park, change uniforms, and play again on behalf of another industrial sponsor. Each player got twenty-five dollars a game, which, typically, was bet with his counterpart on the other team. The winning player at each position would likely make fifty dollars a game; the loser, nothing. He had his nose broken three times in basketball and injured his knee in baseball. Afterward, but still before I was born, my father kept a horse (a stallion, he always insisted), which he rode daily in Chicago's parks. When he married, he took up bowling with a vengeance, and began the harvest of trophies that didn't end until just before he died.

I won't win any of the trophies for this race. But I

am running in it and I will run respectably for an unremarkable man of my age competing in one of his first formal athletic contests. At my age my father had been a champion in four or five sports. He died two years ago. Is it only coincidence that I am suddenly running competitively now?

My memory brings me back to third grade. Spring had melted the last traces of gray ice and snow off the gravel of the Darwin School yard. Johnny O'Brien invites me to play third base in a softball game against another third-grade class. I had not played softball before, but knew most of the rules (like all American boys) and had messed around some with ball and bat on the streets and at family picnics.

That night at dinner I proudly announced that I would be playing third base in the game next day after school. My debut, so to speak, in organized sports.

"You can't play third base!" my father shouted.

"What do you mean?" I protested. "Johnny O'Brien asked me. It's *his* idea."

"I don't care whose idea it is. You can't play third base . . . you're *left-handed!*"

The fierceness with which he offered this unalterable universal principle cannot be imagined. I didn't understand, but I knew it was final, irrevocable.

"Look," he impatiently explained, "if a left-hander fields the ball at third base, he has to turn toward the first baseman before he can throw the batter out."

Of course. No calculation of physiological imperatives had ever before been applied to a game of softball to be played by third-graders on a gravel schoolyard. I said nothing more, had nothing to say. How could I possibly confront Johnny O'Brien with my handicap? My playing career was over. My social life, never robust, was about to end.

"Is there *any* position I *can* play?" Tears were about to brim over.

"Sure—left-handers are great at first base. Tell them you can play first base."

That was it. The subject was dropped. My father assumed the message had been received and would be carried to Johnny O'Brien. I don't remember how I lasted through dinner without dissolving helplessly into tears. I remember thinking that if I let myself go I would seem less the man and the athlete than news of my ridiculous playing defect had already revealed.

The next day I approached Johnny O'Brien before class and tried to explain why his invitation to be third baseman had to be rejected—but, if he pleased, I could play first. In fact, I assured him I would bring special advantages to first base. He was perplexed, which made me feel better about my own confusion over my father's edict. First base, needless to say, was already promised to someone else, who was not interested in the crippling handicap that his right-handedness represented.

I ended up in right field, it being—as always—the place where kids put their team problems. Not a ball was hit to me all day. Quite possibly none of my fellow eight-year-olds hit the ball to the outfield that day, in any direction.

I had had a bad time of it, first when the original game plan in which I was to be a star infielder unraveled and then in the lonely and useless right-field vigil. But I had done the right thing. That night at dinner, I proudly told my father his orders had been followed.

"They should have taken you out of the game," he answered. "When I coach baseball, I yank a guy out if he doesn't watch every play closely, get up on his toes for every pitch."

"I don't understand what you mean, Dad."

"I saw you play right field. You had your hands in your pockets. You just *stood* there."

"How could you have watched me?"

"I drove over and parked in the alley behind the schoolyard. I saw you. You weren't concentrating. You weren't ready for every pitch. That's no way to play baseball."

I got no credit for having relinquished third base, no sympathy for the misery inside me as I stood around in right field, hands in pockets. It was *cold* out there. And why in hell hadn't he said something— "Take your hands out of your pockets," or even, "Good luck," or at least "Hello"—before driving back to his office? He had spied on me.

I am waiting in line for another drink of water, hopping about with four thousand other runners as the start of the twenty-kilometer First Chicago Distance Classic approaches. There is still some cloud cover keeping the temperature down, and no rain threatens. The invited "stars" are beginning to assemble. Frank Shorter arrives, the United States Olympic gold medalist in '72. Shorter is bird-boned like me, and even skinnier. He is taller, however, and looks more like an athlete.

I was always short, sometimes a bit pear-shaped as a kid. Among kids I knew, I would be chosen early when teams were picked, if one or the other team captain wanted a good fielding first baseman who always was up on his toes for the pitch and never put his hands in his pockets. But I couldn't say this to strangers; they wouldn't believe me anyhow. So I often was the last player chosen. It always hurt. During warm-ups I would run my legs off to catch impossible flies and field tricky grounders, partly to show off but also to avoid the bitter sensation of once again being rejected.

Fifteen minutes to the start and the race announcer asks all runners to assemble in Monroe Street, according to their estimated pace. At the front, a big sign displays the number five. Here, world-class runners, Olympic champions including Shorter, take their places, since they are likely to finish the race in an average time of less than five minutes per mile. Twenty-five yards behind, another sign displays a six; twenty-five yards behind that there is a seven. The eight is a full block away from the starting line. With little grumbling, everyone mills through the throng to his or her appropriate spot.

Runners rarely cheat on this arrangement to seek an edge. There is no gain to be gotten. A few yards' advantage will not turn a seven-minute runner into a five-minute winner. The popularity of distance races today attracts crowds of thousands, and approximately 5,300 are starting this race. If faster runners started behind slower ones, accidental but inevitable bumping and tripping would be epidemic, and leave hundreds sprawled on the ground shortly after the starting shot.

George and I enter the street just behind the seven-minute sign—a bit of hubris on my part, but only twenty seconds' worth or so. The crowd is so tight that we cannot bend down. The act of lifting an arm jostles several fellow runners. A sensation of *déjà vu* sweeps over me. Last time I was in a crowd so thick was during the final peace march of the Vietnam war. Then, too, an announcer was marshaling participants, promising that the event was about to begin, urging them not to push, commenting on the large turnout, assuring them about the weather, reviewing the route. Looking around, I wondered how many of my contemporaries in this race were with me seven years ago. Tom Hayden says that the political and social dissidents of the sixties are now selfish seekers of personal gratification. He uses running as an example. Or are we like England's postwar generation? "We made a bad mess of the transition from a nation of brainwashed patriots to a population of in-turned selves," writes John Fowles in his novel *Daniel Martin*. "We then broke up into tribes and classes and finally into private selves." Should I feel guilty? Have I forsaken social reform for private salvation? Or is there some truth in the idea that if we can bring some order and health to our own minds and bodies, we might better serve larger goals?

Is it coincidence that so many of the runners surrounding me this morning cast their first votes for John Kennedy and a bright future, but soon were plunged into the darkness of murder in Mississippi and Vietnam, and fetid corruption in Washington? Since those halcyon days of the early sixties, the world seems to have become impossibly complex and ambiguous, offering nothing but knotty problems that defy solutions. Everybody needs authentic challenges that are simple, sharply defined, and capable of being met. However, life's serious contests have no courses that can be measured. They end in no clearly perceived finish lines. Achievements, when they can be battered out at all, tend to be modest, incremental.

Maybe this race is a metaphor for the way we idealize life. It can provide an "almost moral release," says occasional racer Jamie Kalven. The problem some racers have, though, is that they confuse metaphor and reality. They believe that victory in a race, or a lottery, or a seduction, will resolve the bigger dilemmas. I relish the race for what it is, not a transcendent life victory, but a rare chance to play an enjoyable game with myself.

Finally the race starter tells us there is one minute to go and wishes us good luck. Then the gun goes off and—nothing happens. I am reminded again, literally and figuratively, of the demonstrations of the sixties. This is a whopping big crowd, hard to move; it can't be started all at once. Two thousand runners are in front of me. We watch thirty seconds pass, an eternity, and remain penned in by other bodies. A moment of panic—I am in a race, the gun has fired, and I cannot move! Nightmares come to mind. The wicked witch approaches, but I cannot move; my feet are rooted to the ground.

I see heads way in front, almost imperceptibly at first, begin to bob up and down. Row after row of heads and shoulders are now in motion. Then the thousands of heads have become a sea of waves, slowly undulating. The sound and feel of the herd comes later, like thunder after lightning.

The sea engulfs me and I am swept away, down Monroe Street past Dearborn, past State Street, under the el tracks at Wabash, out of the shadows of skyscrapers at Michigan Avenue. George Vernon darts ahead, gaining lengths on me by broken-field running. Momentarily, I am tempted to follow him, to attempt the whole run at his seven-minute-per-mile pace instead of my anticipated seven-and-a-half-minute average. Then he's gone and I am on my own.

The crowd begins to dissolve, my stride lengthens, and I am racing, past the Art Institute . . . past Buckingham Fountain. The sea of runners has now stretched into a river in front of me, coursing into a right turn at the shore of Lake Michigan. Police have blocked off two southbound lanes of Lake Shore Drive. All of the traffic is now stopped as we cross the other six lanes. The Sunday morning drivers blink in amazement as this motley horde of men and women in their skivvies pours out of the Loop. Wiry athletes, gray-haired cardiac patients, ten-year-old children, couples holding hands, competitors in wheelchairs. Yes, wheelchairs. The Sidewinders' Track Club entered six members in the race. They started off with a fifteen-minute advantage. An hour from now, one of the wheelchair athletes, Randy Wix, will cross the finish line less than two minutes behind Frank Shorter, the winner. Handicaps don't stop dedicated runners. Richard Traum, who has an artificial leg, regularly finishes the New York City marathon. "Here I am," he said, "running twenty-six miles when I never dreamed I could ever run a mile."

At the Field Museum, the river of runners is guided onto the lakefront parkway. It is briefly parallel to another unlikely river of bodies wound around the museum. Thousands spent the night here outside, waiting to see the Treasures of Tutankhamen, and they are entertained in their last hour of impatient shifting from foot to foot by the flow of racers of every description. These two crowds of humanity are not altogether unrelated. The ancient Egyptian word *ka* means the soul, and is also the word for breath. The union of soul and breath is an easy concept for runners to understand.

We pass the first checkpoint. An official calls out the elapsed time—7 minutes, 30 seconds. I am delighted. This is close to what I had hoped to average for the entire 12.4 miles. Then I realize that this seven and a half minutes included at least a minute of waiting time at the start. In fact, I am running too fast; I can't possibly keep up a 6.30 pace. But the runners I am with offer me no incentive to slow down.

The sweat begins to rise. I look around. A girl of eighteen or so is running a bit behind. I judge her to be a seven-minute runner and begin to pace her. We start to pass runners. She is good, and steady. I see my first dropout, panting and walking in the grass just off the course. We pass more disabled runners. Some are stretching their cramped legs in the hope of rejoining the race. Others are stretched out, injured or, more likely, exhausted, not having seriously trained for long-distance racing. I still feel pretty good and am exhilarated by our pace.

I am especially exhilarated by my ability to keep up with an eighteen-year-old girl. When I was a kid, I never could have run a race with a girl. From fourth grade through high school, I had a tomboy classmate—a marvelous athlete, and tough. She would rightly be chosen before me for any sport, which would have caused few problems except that her name—and mine—was Joel. The team captain would call out, "Joel!" I'd step forward. "Uh uh, the *other* Joel." Titters, snorts, giggles. She was a nice person, and I would not have resented her considerable abilities if only she had been named Alice—or Charlie, for that matter. For years I wished my name were Mickey.

We come to the first refreshment stand and I lose my female pacer as almost everybody slows for a cup of water or Gatorade. A boy scout is handing out cups of water. I grab one and resume a full pace, trying to swallow a few mouthfuls without spilling the water or biting my tongue or—a real danger—choking on it. Maybe half gets down before I add my crumpled cup to the littered landscape.

On my own now, I feel tenseness in my neck and downward to my legs. I use a simple yoga technique to loosen up that involves relaxing the jaw. As soon as my attention focuses there, I feel the tightness and begin to concentrate on dissolving it. I quiet my thoughts about the seven and a half miles to go, the excitement of racing, the anticipation of finishing, and the fear of not finishing. Just let the jaw relax. It does, and I do, as if the jaw were the center of all the body's tightness and strain, and I begin moving pretty well.

The tension of athletic effort almost did me in as a kid. For example, it prevented me from standing up straight as I walked out onto the swimming pier at Mohawk Lodge on the day of my swimming test. The two piers were twenty-five yards apart and I had to swim the distance—without stopping. We had only been at camp three weeks. Swimming lessons had taught me the strokes, but had not given me the confidence at age seven to swim that distance, on the deep side of the rope barrier, with the swimming counselors watching.

I jumped in at their instruction and started to dog-paddle. Keeping my head out of the water was work enough. Paddling five yards took my breath away. The next five yards were hard, but I was still OK. Then I discovered that breathing was no longer possible without great effort. It wouldn't come. I panicked, making breathing even harder. Five more yards, I could barely see except that the pier ahead began to spin away. I was getting dizzy, flailing erratically, paddling off course. Mustering all my remaining strength, more than I knew I had, I brought the pier back in front of me and somehow splashed out a few more strokes. My lungs were on fire. Rapid and painful gasps replaced breathing, unnatural sounds that frightened everybody within earshot. Five yards to go. No coordination, just will, the need to pass the test. I was so close to the pier, but also close to drowning. Finally, it was only the need to survive that brought me to my goal. I grabbed the ladder and hung there gasping and wheezing. I had done it. The little plywood plaque, shining with shellac, my name burned into it, would be presented to me. I could swim.

I couldn't have done it if *he* had been there. *He* had always taken risks; he thought risks were something for him to take as a kid making it up out of the slums. He saw his job as a father to keep me from risks: Don't go out too far. Don't overdo it. Don't take chances. Choose survival over life. Growing up, I thought he was right; at least, I complied.

Twelve years after I got my swimming plaque, I was swimming beyond the breakers in Acapulco Bay. I turned around to come in and saw my father standing at the water's edge. I couldn't hear him, but he had obviously been calling me, was angry because I swam out so far and failed to heed his instructions to return. Before a conscious thought could form, I turned again, out to sea, and raced away for a quarter mile, further than I would otherwise have gone. Finally, I turned, lazily swam in, rolling and floating, preparing to absorb his anger, preferring that to his dominance. From that time on, I began trying to live closer to the edge, further from the shore, often ordered back by him, tortured by my warring impulses to go over the edge in retaliation and simultaneously wanting to stay close, to be protected.

The monitor calls out my time for four miles at a reasonable twenty-nine minutes. Just then, the thin but steady line of runners in front of me is shifting to the right side of the course and I hear them applauding. I see a policeman coming at us on a three-wheeled motorbike followed by . . . Frank Shorter! He has been to the turnaround and is coming back toward the finish. And he's beautiful to watch. An easy gliding pace. He seems not to be sweating at all, not even touching the ground. His speed is astounding; suddenly my twenty-nine minutes for four miles seems glacial.

We applaud him, thrilled by his performance, thrilled to be in the same race, to know enough about the sport to *appreciate* his ability. It's like pianists with some modest talent listening to Horowitz. By watching the masters we derive standards against which to measure ourselves. How much greater my appreciation is for Shorter's artistry now that I've raced with him. I had seen him run on television, without experiencing anywhere near the same level of understanding and respect for his achievement.

Before the excitement of Shorter's appearance has diminished, I hear even louder applause, and then Randy Wix passes, hot on Shorter's heels, the spokes of his wheelchair humming as his powerful arms propel the wheels at breakneck speed. And soon Kim Merritt comes by. She is applauded by us because she is a woman, setting a hot pace. We didn't know then that she was in the process of breaking the women's world record at this distance by a full minute and twenty-seven seconds.

I run easily for the next couple of miles, exhilarated by Shorter and Merritt and the wheelchair challengers. After completing the arc of the turnaround, I see Tom Boodell, a law school classmate, watching the race with his family. They call out support. A pleasant surprise. For the first time I notice other spectators lining the race course. This is a *public* event! The feel of the crowd has always been important to me—on stage in college; in lecture halls, courtrooms, and TV studios. But I hadn't thought of the public aspect of this race until Tom waved to me. I have been largely unconscious of the audience, lost in my participation. The run and the race are a means of developing myself through performance, without demanding that I be a performer.

Another water station looms. I maneuver close enough to snatch a cup, drink three or four gulps, pour the rest over my head, and fling it. The last swallow sticks in my throat, causing a few choking coughs—not serious, I know, but several runners around me interpret them as incipient exhaustion or worse. "Only a couple of miles to go!" "Easy fella, you'll make it!" "Go for it, man, almost there now!" In fact there are more than three miles to go, but I'm OK, happy to be in good company, the camaraderie of the contestants.

This, I remind myself, is a sports contest, but one in which the "competition" nurses you along psychologically and physically. Not like my brief interlude with squash at Harvard. As a kid, I had developed a style of scorekeeping in games like tennis and squash that was violently at odds with the eastern prep school manner that Chris Anderson (now, under his real name, an editor of a hip magazine) had adopted. In Chicago, we called out the score after each point. It was the easiest way to remember it. I had not been at Harvard long enough to appreciate the sensibilities of the budding gentleman class. They found repeated mention of the score to be aggressive, hostile, and uncivil. Not to say they didn't want to win—just that they were trained to be quiet about it.

One afternoon, I was doing pretty well against Anderson, game after game. "Three-nothing . . . five-two . . . eight-three . . . fourteen-nine . . . game!!" One game for me, then a second. Anderson's gorge rose, until a strangled shout came from his throat and his racket screamed through the air, shattering against the wall. He advanced on me as if to kill, forgetting that I was the only one left with a racket—not much of a weapon but better than nothing. He stormed off the court. A mutual friend explained it that night. Anderson, it seemed, had been seething about my poker-playing style, too. Lots of patter and commentary on the relative values of my cards and everybody else's. Such aggresiveness, even in fun, is not much valued at Andover, Exeter, and St. Paul's. I hardly ever call out the score anymore.

The race marshal calls out—not the score, but the time at ten miles. One hour, eighteen minutes. Not too bad, but not as good as I had hoped. I am averaging just under eight minutes per mile, when I had hoped to do the race in closer to a seven-minute average. I pull abreast of a man about my size. He steps up the pace a bit. I move with him.

In my first race, a ten-miler, I began to develop cramps about two miles from the finish. Now I take inventory. No cramps, my gut feels fine. The weather continues to be good—no direct sun, and the temperature is still no more than 75 degrees. At the same stage last time out, the heat and sun had begun to affect me. Finally, I mentally examine my fragile feet. I recently was fitted with new, lighter orthotic appliances, and, to my delight and relief, they are working fine.

It occurs to me that I can do still better and I step out, exchanging encouraging words with my erstwhile buddy. I pass more runners, twenty-five or so. A bearded contestant seems to be going about the same pace. We lock strides. "Let's go for it," I say as we pass the eleven-mile mark—one and a half to go. He smiles and we begin to run in earnest. I am now pushing against the limit, testing myself in the struggle that the Greeks called "agon" (from which comes our "agony").

My breathing changes from the smooth two counts in, two counts out, that has sustained me nicely throughout the race. It is not as labored as when I swam my test at Mohawk Lodge, and in no danger of becoming so. I am in better condition now than ever before in my life. Reassuringly, I remember Nina Kuscsik's comment yesterday that even champions like her lose the rhythm of their breathing when they go into their final "kicks."

I'm high. My life is significantly improving at an age when the lives of many classmates and colleagues seem to be disintegrating. Ahead of me, running much faster than I can, are Dr. Sheehan, age fifty-eight, Ray Sears, age seventy-one, Hal Higdon, age forty-six; and the marvelous women, Miki Gorman, age forty-one, Nina Kuscsik, age thirty-eight, and Dr. Joan Ullyot, my age exactly. This is fun! I want to be racing like this in twenty years; only maybe then I'll get down to seven minutes or less per mile. I don't want to race every week, only a couple times a year, so that racing does not consume my life but adds a special little perk to it

Everybody runs his own race. Hal Higdon, who wrote *Fitness After Forty*, told a story yesterday about another runner over forty, Dr. Morton Pastor.

They met two weeks after both had run the Mission Bay marathon. "How'd you do?" Higdon asked Pastor. "Well, I ran four hours, thirty-six minutes, but I was first in my class." Realizing that Pastor's time would have resulted in a Frank Shorter lapping him if the race were run on a two-lap course, an incredulous Higdon asked him what class that was. Pastor answered, "Anesthesiologists over forty with seven daughters."

We make the jog around the front of the Shedd Aquarium and straighten out to run the last one-half mile, downhill to the Buckingham Fountain. Here, the course is lined with spectators. They have taken over the job of urging us on, now that we are too exhausted and running too hard to do it for one another. We accelerate and run into a chute lined with spectators. They are clapping for us, for all of us, for the scores in view, for the hundreds who have finished and the thousands who will finish. And then—we are being told to slow down. Slow down! There are fifty yards to go, but the First National Bank's highly touted racing computer has broken down and is not recording the finishers' times as fast as they are finishing! We are all arriving simultaneously. We slow . . . we stop, as a line of gasping, sweating runners blocks our way. My new friend, bless his heart, is equipped with a wrist-style stopwatch. He shuts it down. One hour and thirty-two minutes. I wait longer to "officially" cross the finish line than I had waited to start running after the "official" start of the race.

But none of this matters. I have finished—in respectable time—and, incredibly, feel terrific. *Agon* has yielded to ecstasy. After making my way to the finish line, I search out my wife in the huge, happy crowd of runners and their families. We find George Vernon, who finished ten or fifteen minutes ago, and we all have a delightful drink of tea and orange juice. "Damn it, George," I shout, "I feel terrific. Let's run the course again and make it a marathon!" He remains sprawled on the grass. He has run several marathons and knows that our current level of training can sustain twenty kilometers but not twenty-six miles.

I shuck my shoes. Dr. Sheehan and his wife come over and we share our jug of tea and lemonade with them. He looks at my feet and, on a busman's holiday, comments on my extraordinary display of forefoot varus, visible to him even at a casual glance. Bless these feet, however they may twist and slant; today they performed like heroes. Not a hint of pain or numbness. In fact, I find that this, my best performance, will yield less aches and stiffness in the next couple of days than many shorter, slower training runs. Maybe I was running better for running a bit faster. Or maybe the extra few miles of training in the past month paid off.

An uncommon scene now is unfolding at the finish line. Bob DeYoung is completing his race, holding one end of a shirt while runner Tom Pawlik holds the other end and finishes just in front. DeYoung is blind. He ran today with the help of his friends, Tom and John Pawlik.

We collect towels, cups, warm-up clothes, and walk slowly to the car. As we motor along Lake Shore Drive, now two and a half hours after the start of the race, a thousand joggers are still chugging toward the finish, including Dr. Noel Nequin's team of heart attack patients from the Cardiac Rehabilitation Center. We give them friendly toots of the car horn. We pass runners for miles, almost back to the race turnaround.

To get here, all of us overcame some handicap,

even though it might not be as evident as DeYoung's, or wheelchair champion Randy Wix's. All of us have chosen life over survival. I pray for all the rest to finish and to feel—at their finish—as magnificent as I do now.

Bibliography

Books

Adams, Henry. *The Education of Henry Adams.* New York: The Modern Library, 1918.

Bannister, Roger. *Four-Minute Mile.* New York: Dodd, Mead, 1955.

Barfield, Owen. *Saving the Appearances: A Study in Idolatry.* New York: Harcourt Brace Jovanovich, 1963.

Benson, Herbert, M.D. *The Relaxation Response.* New York: William Morrow, 1975.

Cooper, Kenneth H., M.D. *Aerobics.* New York: Bantam Books, 1968.

Cox, Harvey. *Turning East: The Promise and Peril of the New Orientalism.* New York: Simon & Schuster, 1977.

David-Neel, Alexandra. *Magic and Mystery in Tibet.* New York: Penguin Books, 1971.

Gardiner, E. Norman. *Athletics of the Ancient World.* London: Oxford University Press, 1930.

Herrigel, Eugen. *Zen in the Art of Archery.* New York: Pantheon Books, 1964.

Jackson, Ian. *Yoga and the Athlete.* Mountain View, California: World Publications, 1975.

Kostrubala, Thaddeus, M.D. *The Joy of Running.* Philadelphia: J. B. Lippincott, 1976.

Leonard, George. *The Ultimate Athlete.* New York: Viking Press, 1974.

Pennington, Campbell, W., *The Tarahumar of Mexico: Their Environment and Material Culture.* Salt Lake City: University of Utah Press, 1963.

Rama, Ballentine and Ajaya. *Yoga and Psychotherapy: The Evolution of Consciousness.* Glenview, Illinois: Himalayan Institute, 1976.

Rohe, Fred. *The Zen of Running.* New York: Random House, 1975.

Sagan, Carl. *The Dragons of Eden: Speculations on the Evolution of Human Intelligence.* New York: Random House, 1977.

Schoolboys of Barbiana. *Letter to a Teacher.* New York: Vintage Books, 1971.

Sheehan, George A., M.D. *Dr. Sheehan on Running.* Mountain View, California: World Publications, 1975.

Smith, Adam. *Powers of Mind.* New York: Random House, 1975.

Smith, Nathan J., M.D. *Food for Sport.* Palo Alto, California: Ball Publishing Co., 1976.

Spino, Mike. *Beyond Jogging: The Innerspaces of Running.* New York: Berkley Publishing Corp., 1976.

Subotnick, Steven I., D.P.M. *The Running Foot Doctor.* Mountain View, California: World Publications, 1977.

Ullyot, Joan, M.D. *Women's Running.* Mountain View, California: World Publications, 1976.

Williams and Speryn. *Sports Medicine*. Baltimore: Williams & Wilkins Co., 1976.

Articles

Costill, D. L. "Nutritional Requirements for Endurance Athletes." Unpublished paper, *Human Performance Laboratory*, Ball State University (Muncie, Indiana).

Davidson and Kripper. "Biofeedback Research: The Data and Their Implications," *Biofeedback and Self-Control: An Aldine Reader in the Regulation of Bodily Processes and Consciousness*. Edited by Theodore X. Barber et al. Chicago: Aldine, 1972.

Gallico, Paul. "The Feel," *Farewell to Sport*. Edited by Paul Gallico. Plainview, New York: Books for Libraries, 1970, p. 287.

Goldstein and Brady. "Biofeedback Heart Rate Training During Exercise." *Biofeedback and Self-Regulation*. New York: Plenum Press, Vol. 2, No. 2 (June, 1977).

Ismail, A. H., and Trachtman, L. E. "Jogging the Imagination." *Psychology Today* (March, 1973), p. 79.

Madhua, K. W. "Studies in Alveolar Air." *Yoga-Mimosa*, Vol. 6 (1956), p. 99.

Pelletier, Wilfred, "Childhood in an Indian Village," *This Book Is About Schools*. Edited by Satu Repo. New York: Vintage Books, 1970, p. 20.

Swinn, Richard M. "Body Thinking: Psychology for

Olympic Champs." *Psychology Today*, Vol. 10, No. 2 (July, 1976), p. 38.

Szent-Gyoergyi, Albert. "Drive in Living Matter to Perfect Itself." *Synthesis*, Vol. 1, No. 1 (1976), p. 14.

Index

About the Author

Joel Henning is a lawyer and writer who lives with his wife and three daughters in Chicago. He graduated from Harvard College and Harvard Law School, has been a consultant to Ralph Nader and a fellow of the Adlai Stevenson Institute of International Affairs.